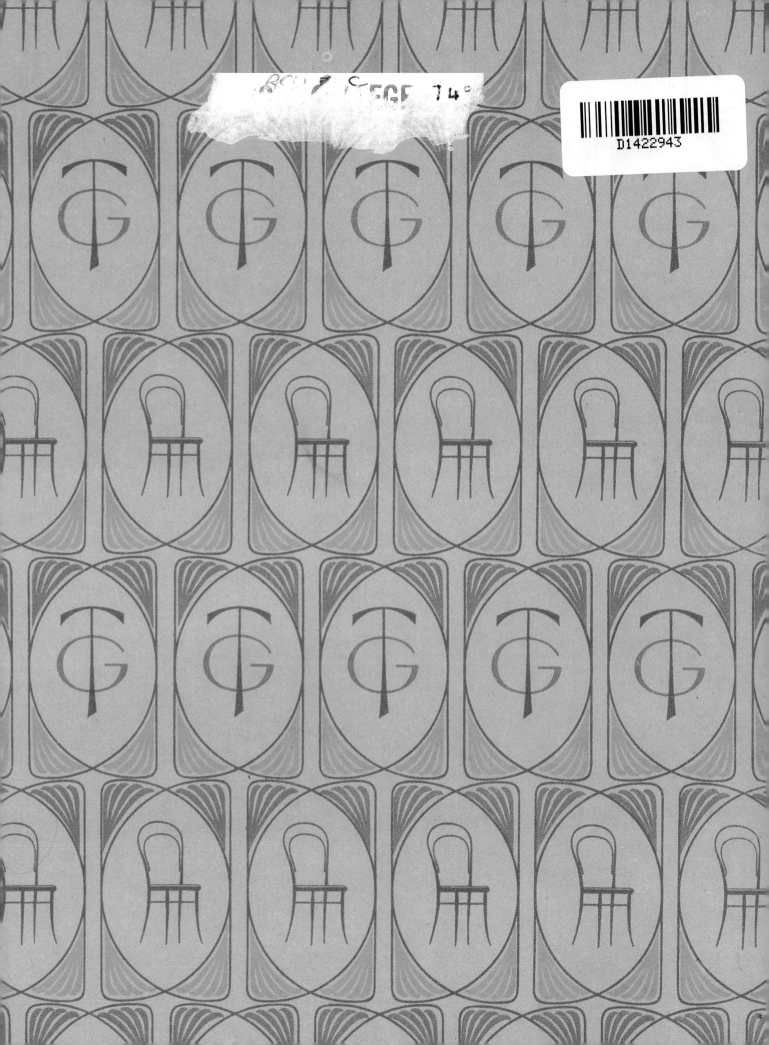

THONET

THONET

Classic Furniture in Bent Wood and Tubular Steel

Alexander von Vegesack

with text by
Brigitta Pauley
and
Peter Ellenberg

HAZAR
P·U·B·L·I·S·H·I·N·G

FRONTISPIECE:

As a sales feature, especially for the overseas export market,
Thonet claimed that 36 chairs could be packed into 1 cubic metre.

Published 1996 by Hazar Publishing Ltd.
147 Chiswick HighRoad, London W4 2DT

A catalogue record of this title is available
from the British Library

ISBN 1 874371 26 1

Based on DAS THONET BUCH
By Alexander von Vegesack and Dr Albrecht Bangert
Published by Bangert Verlag Munchen 1987

Picture research by Serge Mauduit
Edited by Marie Clayton
Designed by Robert Mathias, Publishing Workshop

Colour separation by Dot 'n Line (Aust) Pty Ltd

Contents

Chronology

1796	**2nd July** Michael Thonet is born in Boppard on the Rhine
1819	Thonet opens his own furniture workshop at the age of 23
1820	Thonet marries Anna Maria Grahs
c1836	The Boppard chair, Thonet's first chair in laminated veneer, is developed
1840	**17th Oct** Application for a patent in Berlin is refused
1841	Application for a French patent is accepted Thonet exhibits bent wood pieces at the Koblenz Fair, which attract the attention of Prince Klemens von Metternich, the Austrian Chancellor
1842	1st Austrian patent is granted, probably due to Prince Metternich's influence. Boppard workshop is seized by creditors Thonet moves to Vienna with his family Thonet and sons work with Clemens List, producing a simple version of the Boppard chair.
1843	The Thonets work for Carl Leistler on parquet flooring for the Palais Liechtenstein. The Liechtenstein chair is developed
1847	1st Austrian patent expires
1849	Thonet and his sons open their own workshop at Hauptstraße 396 in Gumpendorf

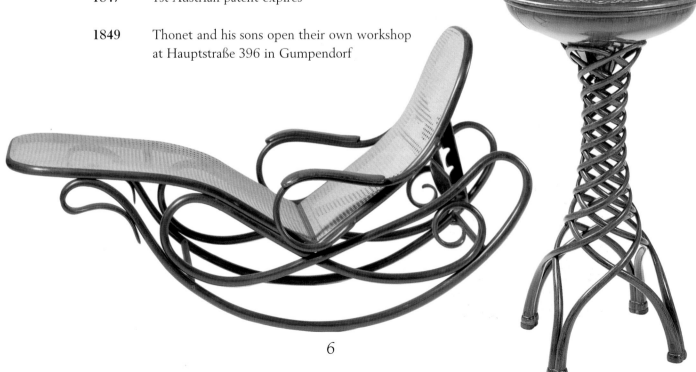

1850   The Schwarzenberg chair (model no. 1) and the Cafe Daum chair (model no. 4) are developed

1851   Thonet exhibits at the Great Exhibition at Crystal Palace and wins a bronze medal

1852   **28th July** 2nd Austrian patent is granted
The first retail shop is opened in Vienna

1853   **1st Nov** Gebrüder Thonet is founded
A new workshop is opened at Mollardgasse in Vienna

1854   Thonet sends mass-produced pieces to the Munich Industrial Fair

1855   Thonet exhibits win a silver medal at the Paris Exposition Universelle
8th July Gebrüder Thonet receives the authority to run a factory, which frees the company from the restraints of the guilds.

1856   **17th June** Austrian nationality granted to Thonet and his sons
3rd Austrian patent, to bend solid wood, is granted

1857   Authorisation to produce furniture, parquet flooring and other wood items is granted
The first factory, at Koritschan, is opened

1858   Vienna workshop is closed, and all production is moved to Koritschan
A new sales branch is opened in the prime location of Stephansplatz in Vienna

1859-60   1st broadsheet catalogue is issued
The Consumer chair (model no. 14) is developed

1861   The second factory at Bistritz is opened

1865	A country seat at Nagyugrócz is purchased, which later becomes a factory
1867	The Demonstration chair is first exhibited at the Paris Exposition Universelle Wsetin factory is opened
1869	3rd patent expires and a host of competitors enter the field
1871	**3rd March** Michael Thonet dies
1880	Novo-Radomsk factory is opened in Polish Russia
1883	The Rocking sofa (model no. 7500) is developed
1889	Frankenberg factory is opened
1899	A limestone factory is founded to produce building materials for factories and houses.
1902-3	The Vienna Chair (model no. 9) is developed
1905	The Postsparkassen stool, designed by Otto Wagner, is launched
1906-7	The Three Legged Chair, (model no. 81) is developed
1912	Thonet reaches its top output of 1.8 million pieces per year
1913	The International Construction Industry Fair at Leipzig includes a Thonet Pavilion
1919	Thonet Frères in Paris and Thonet Brothers in New York are founded
1921	Gebrüder Thonet becomes a joint stock company, Thonet AG
1922	Thonet Germany and Thonet Austria become two independent companies
1923	All the Thonet companies merge with Kohn-Mundus to form Thonet-Mundus AG, the world's largest furniture manufacturer
1925	Model no. B3, later known as the Wassily, is developed
1928	The Le Corbusier Chaise Longue (model no. B306), designed by Le Corbusier and his associates Pierre Jeanneret and Charlotte Perriand, is manufactured by Thonet
1929	Thonet-Mundus takes over Standard Möbel
1930	Marcel Breuer's Double Cantilever Chair (model no. B35) is first introduced The Frankenberg factory begins to manufacture tubular steel furniture

1931	Leopold Pilzer becomes the major shareholder of Thonet-Mundus and moves the official headquarters of the company to Switzerland
1932	Mies van der Rohe's Cantilever Chair (model no. MR533), designed in 1927, is now manufactured by Thonet
1936	Pilzer begins to move the company to the USA
1938	Pilzer moves to the USA and sells the Eastern European and German factories back to the Thonet family. Gebrüder Thonet has the markets east of the Rhine, while Thonet-Mundus keeps the rights for America, France and England.
1939	Thonet Industries USA is formed and the Kohn-Mundus name is phased out in the USA.
1941	Thonet Industries USA begin manufacturing Thonet bent wood chairs in Statesville, North Carolina A second factory is opened in Sheboygan, Wisconsin
1945	**12th March** The Gebrüder Thonet factory in Frankenberg is bombed by the Allies Thonet Bentply is introduced by Thonet Industries USA
1949	Gebrüder Thonet rebuilds the Frankenberg factory and produces its first post-war catalogue
1951	Thonet Brothers Ltd in London is closed down by the American company. Thonet Frères in Paris becomes independent
1954	In Czechoslovakia the Thonet company is now state owned and becomes Ton
1962	Thonet Frères is sold to its manager, André Leclerc Thonet Brothers Inc. (USA) is sold to Simmons and Gebrüder Thonet in Germany takes over the rights to the Gebrüder Thonet trademark for Germany and the other EEC countries.
1963	Gebrüder Thonet AG Vienna in Austria, which is still a separate company to Gebrüder Thonet AG in Germany, opens a new modern factory in Friedberg
1978	Gebrüder Thonet AG becomes a private limited company, Gebrüder Thonet GmbH
1979	Simmons, including Thonet Industries, is sold to Gulf and Western
1980	A Thonet Museum is opened in Frankenberg
1985	Thonet Industries is taken over by Manfred Steinfeld, who also owns Shelby Williams Industries

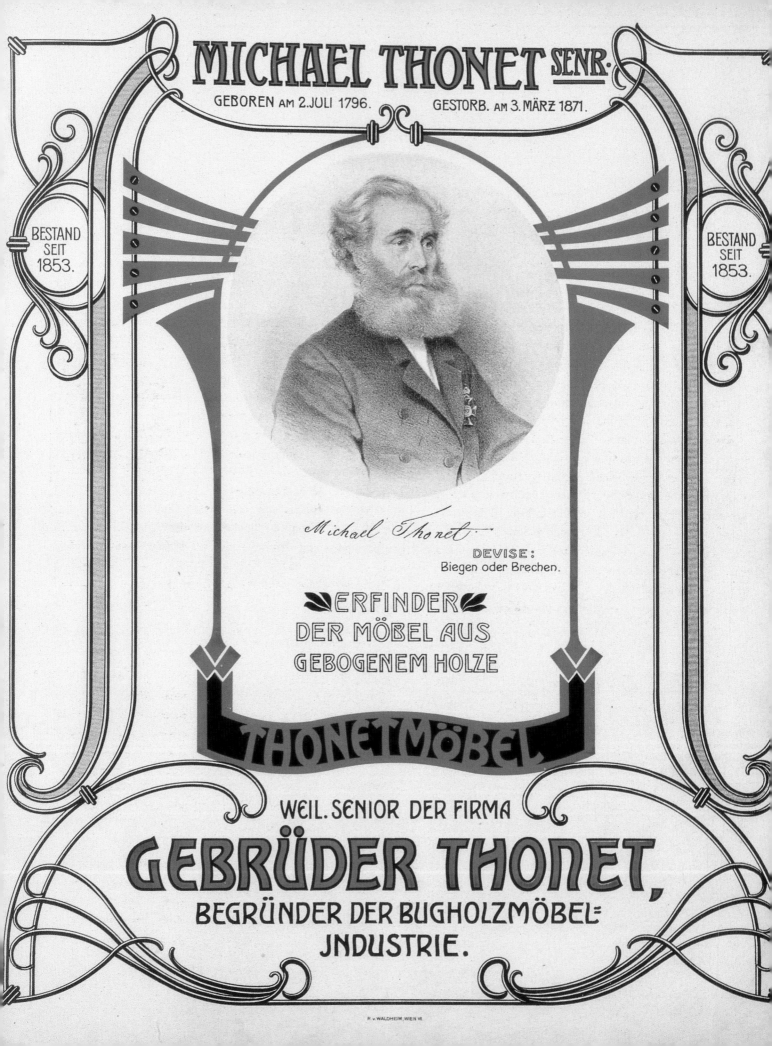

MICHAEL THONET SENR.

GEBOREN AM 2. JULI 1796.   GESTORB. AM 3. MÄRZ 1871.

BESTAND SEIT 1853.

BESTAND SEIT 1853.

Michael Thonet

DEVISE:
Biegen oder Brechen.

ERFINDER DER MÖBEL AUS GEBOGENEM HOLZE

THONETMÖBEL

WEIL. SENIOR DER FIRMA

GEBRÜDER THONET,

BEGRÜNDER DER BUGHOLZMÖBEL=
JNDUSTRIE.

R. v. WALDHEIM, WIEN VI.

A Family Concern

When Michael Thonet died on March 3rd 1871, surrounded by his large family, he was the most important furniture manufacturer of the 19th century and a world famous man. He had been born 75 years earlier on July 2nd 1796 in Boppard on the Rhine, the only son of a poor family that had moved to the area ten years earlier. His father was a tanner but Michael, in the hope of bettering himself, was apprenticed to a cabinet maker. In 1819, aged 23, Michael Thonet opened his own furniture workshop and a year later married Anna Maria Grahs, the daughter of a local butcher. Over the next ten years they had four sons: Franz, Michael, August and Josef. A fifth son, Jakob, was born much later in 1841. Michael Thonet's reputation as a skilful and quality-conscious cabinet maker soon spread beyond Boppard and his four older sons became actively involved in their father's growing workshop, which produced fairly plain furniture in the late Biedermeier style using high-quality cherry wood, pear wood and mahogany veneer. In keeping with the zeitgeist, Thonet seems to have been very interested in flowing contours and incorporated swinging volutes and carved rosettes into his work. Initially all Michael Thonet's furniture was manufactured using traditional methods: his beds and settees were built entirely in the conventional manner - not even the decorations, despite their appearance, were made of bent wood.

ABOVE: *Michael Thonet's five sons, (clockwise from top) August, Josef, Michael, Jakob and Franz.*

LEFT: *This early settee from Michael Thonet's Boppard workshop does not point to his experiments with bending wood. Despite their appearance, all parts - including the decorations - were carved in the traditional manner.*

OPPOSITE: *An illustration in the 1904 catalogue, which proclaims Michael Thonet as the 'inventor of bent wood furniture' and says his motto is 'to bend or to break'.*

LEFT: *The English Windsor chair, dating from the 17th century, already integrates pieces of bent wood.*

The search for new techniques

Bending wood was not an innovative idea by Michael Thonet. The Egyptians and the Greeks already knew how to bend wood, using its natural elasticity by exposing one side of a wet piece of wood to fire. This technique was mainly used in ship building. Bent wood furniture had already appeared in the 17th century in the form of the English Windsor chair and it was in England that the first patent applications were filed. The wood was bent by boiling, steaming or exposing directly to fire, all methods more usually applied to ship building than to furniture making. By the 19th century, efforts to rationalise the process of bending wood for the production of furniture, wheels, spiral staircases and window frames had intensified: the Belgian Jean-Joseph Chapuis was building chairs out of laminated bent wood in 1805, the American Samuel Gragg patented his 'elastic chair' made of solid bent wood in 1808, the English craftsman Isaac Sargent became famous for his spiral staircases and Thonet built cartwheels for the Prussian army in the 1840s.

As bent wood seemed a promising technique, both in Europe and the United States, Michael Thonet soon moved away from traditional furniture production and began to develop his technique of laminating wood, which is now regarded as an important experimental phase in the development of the solid wood bending process.

LEFT: *Samuel Gragg (1772-1855) from Boston was granted a US patent in 1808 for his 'elastic chair' made out of solid bent wood.*

LEFT: *This Boppard armchair was made between 1836 and 1842 out of bent laminated veneer in the late Biedermeier style.*

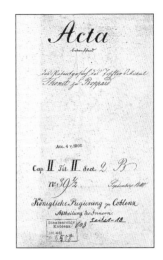

The Boppard furniture

When Michael Thonet started to experiment, he began by cutting wood along the grain into thin veneer strips, which he then boiled in glue and bent in wooden moulds. These very broad strips were cut lengthways into several identical pieces. The chairs he built out of these laminated veneer bundles were not only revolutionary in design but also documented Thonet's constructive innovation, which effortlessly combined form and technique. These chairs, known as his 'Boppard furniture', founded Michael Thonet's reputation; they were light but strong and stylistically in tune with the demands of his clientèle.

All the chairs were identical, which indicates that they were already constructed as part of a standardised mini series which was rationally produced with Thonet's bending forms. From the first, Thonet appears to have had a vision of factory-produced furniture. A shining example of this was already provided in the shape of the nearby Roentgen furniture manufacturers who, with their branches in Paris, Berlin and St. Petersburg, were already legendary as a result of their pioneering work in standardisation and rationalisation.

Thonet's first patent applications

As his furniture grew ever more popular, Thonet was anxious to protect his production process by patent that would help hold competition at bay - although it did necessitate the publication of the technique. On October 17th 1840 the building inspector Claudius von Lessaulx supported Thonet's application for a patent for his bent laminated veneers. The application was denied in Berlin, however, on the grounds that Thonet's method of bending wood was not new and his idea of adding a metal strip to the wood that was to be bent to prevent it splitting did not in itself qualify as an invention.

Despite his success, Thonet did not have the capital to make further patent applications abroad until a group of Boppard businessmen provided him with a loan. Patents were apparently granted in France, Belgium and England, although only the French patent, which was issued in the name of Thonet's financier van Meerten and described the method and its advantages at great length, can now be traced. Unfortunately Thonet was unable to make use of his patents commercially because they were either conditional on his taking part in the manufacturing process or the offers he received were too low.

ABOVE: *Illustration from the American catalogue of 1906/7.*

ABOVE: *Michael Thonet's first application for a patent, which dates from 1840, was turned down by the Prussian Government because the technique was not regarded as innovative.*

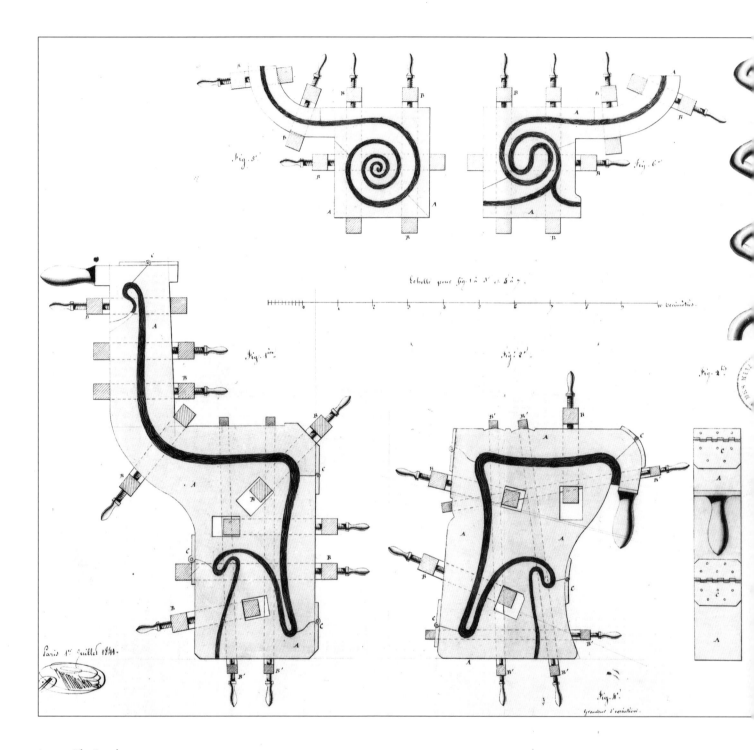

ABOVE: *The French patent
application of 1841 was not
filed by Michael Thonet, but
by his financier van Meerten.
Thonet demonstrated his
new technique for laminated
veneer chairs.*

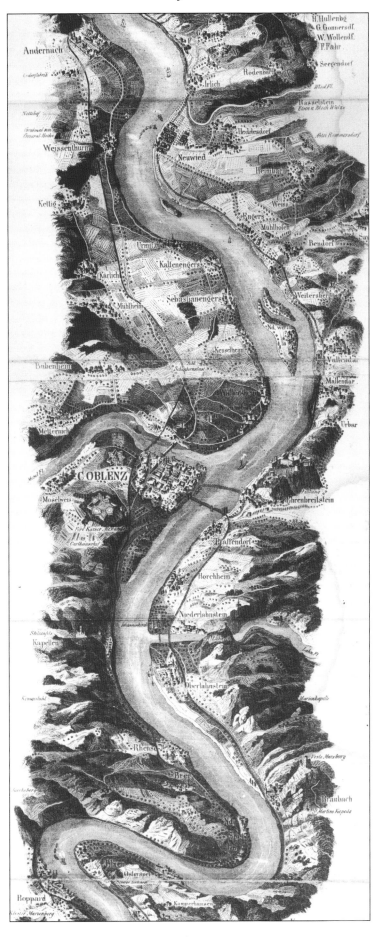

LEFT: *The Rhine from Andernach to Boppard, late last century.*

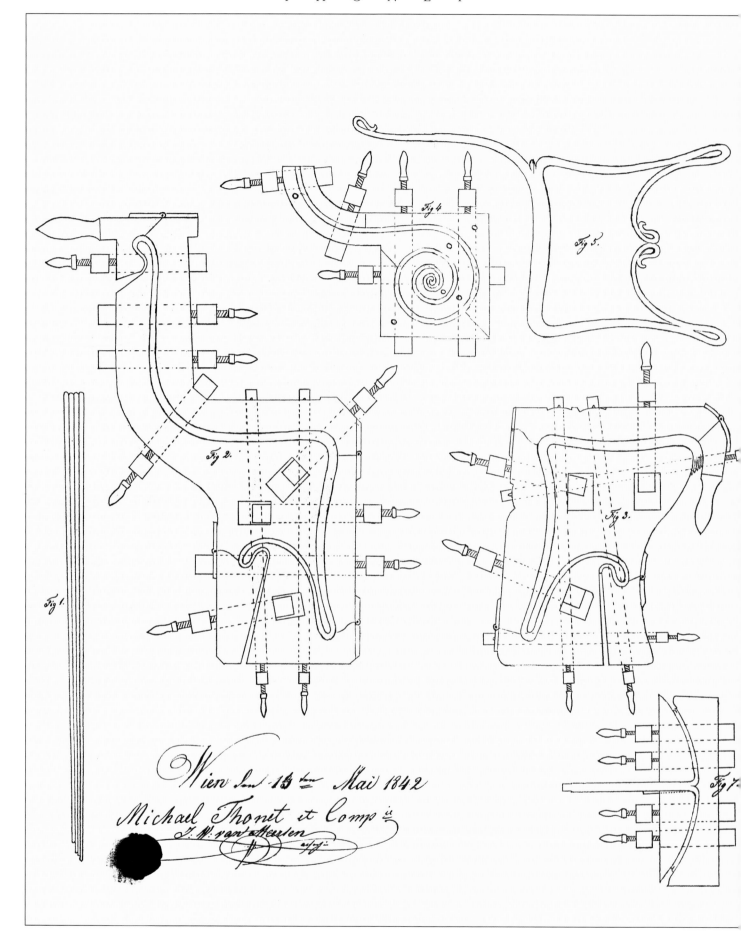

Wien den 13ten Mai 1842

Michael Thonet et Comp:

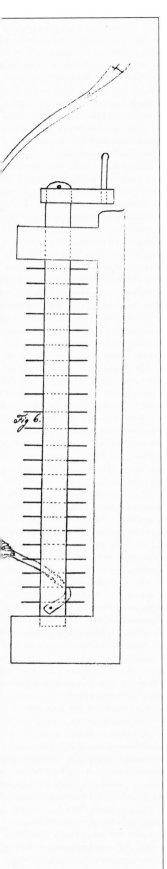

Thonet's meeting with Metternich

As art and craft fairs began to play an important part in communicating technical and structural developments, Thonet decided to introduce his innovative furniture to the public and began exhibiting locally. In the summer of 1841 his elegant bent wood pieces were admired at the Koblenz fair, where they attracted the attention of Prince Klemens von Metternich, the Chancellor of the Austro-Hungarian Empire. Thonet was invited to his castle on the Rhine at Johannisberg and arrived with chairs, a walking stick, a wagon wheel and other bent wood items, which were applauded by the Prince. He is supposed to have encouraged Thonet by saying: 'You will always remain a poor man in Boppard. Go to Vienna, where I shall recommend you to the Court. The journey will cost you nothing as you can travel from Frankfurt to Vienna with the Imperial courier'.

It would be wrong to assume that Thonet was overjoyed and immediately accepted Metternich's offer; indeed, only five weeks before his departure he placed an advertisement in the local Koblenz paper looking for 5-6 cabinet maker journeymen for his workshop. Nevertheless, in May 1842 Thonet left his family in Boppard and travelled to Vienna. The journey probably does not signify any intention to relocate to Vienna on Thonet's part, but is more likely to have been part of a tactical ploy to use Metternich's influence to gain the coveted 'privilege' (the Austrian version of a patent) for his invention, which he would then sell on to another furniture manufacturer. Metternich enthusiastically arranged for samples of Thonet's work to be shown to the Emperor through his Court Marshall, Baron von Hügel. 'Baron von Hügel notified me,' Thonet wrote in a letter to his family, 'that the Emperor liked the pieces very much indeed and wished to keep some of them'.

Patent politics in Vienna

Thonet's most important financial backer from Boppard, van Meerten, soon arrived in Vienna and began to act as his associate. The regional trade association refused to recognise the innovation and advantages of Thonet's techniques, however - the expert's report argued that bending wood was not of itself innovatory and that the 'chemico-mechanical process' could not be judged because Thonet and van Meerten refused to describe it. The application of 1841 for the French patent had explained that 'chemico' meant boiling the laminates in glue and 'mechanical' referred to the addition of the metal strip to prevent the wood splitting, but by this point Thonet and van Meerten appear to have been trying to keep the process secret again. Nevertheless, on July 16th 1842, Thonet was surprisingly granted a patent 'to bend any, even the most brittle, types of wood into forms and curves by chemico-mechanical means'. Prince Metternich's influence had clearly been crucial and Thonet was well aware of this. It also seems that Thonet's main intention in Vienna from the first was to avoid the restrictions of the guilds and proceed with his vision of mass-production.

LEFT: *The 1842 patent application in Vienna was signed by Michael Thonet himself and surprisingly approved, probably because of Metternich's intervention.*

RIGHT: *This simple version of a Boppard chair was manufactured by Thonet in Vienna while he was working for Clemens List.*

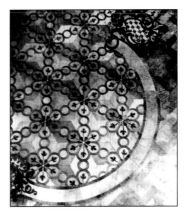

LEFT & DETAILS: *Intricate parquet flooring, consisting of thousands of pieces of different types of bent wood, made by Michael Thonet for the Palais Liechtenstein in Vienna in 1843.*

Problems in Boppard

While Thonet was involved in these patent politics in Vienna, a catastrophe was brewing in Boppard. His creditors had become nervous and forced his wife to sell all the Thonet family property - even a delivery of furniture destined for the Austrian Court was seized. Michael Thonet's reputation in Boppard had sunk so low by 1842 that it is said that no-one would even have lent him a pound of salt, but he nevertheless went on to be one of the most successful factory owners of the age. Thonet probably never returned to Boppard after he assumed Austrian nationality in 1856, although he did continue to employ cabinet makers who had worked for him in his home town.

A fresh start in Vienna

After losing his company and all his property in Boppard, the penniless Thonet moved his family - which now included his fifth son, one-year-old Jakob - to Vienna in 1842. As he was unable to work independently using his patent due to his financial troubles, Thonet and his older sons began to work for the Viennese furniture manufacturer Clemens List in Gumpendorf, producing a simpler version of the Boppard chair. List wanted to retire and sell his business, but he was able to introduce the Thonets to the fashionable English avant-garde architect Peter Hubert Desvignes, who was very taken with Thonet's new techniques. Desvignes supported Thonet and found the family work manufacturing the intricate parquet flooring for the renovation of the prestigious Palais Liechtenstein, which he had been commissioned to undertake. This work had unfortunately already been offered to the flooring manufacturer

ISLE COLLEGE
RESOURCES CENTRE

ABOVE: *When the Palais Liechtenstein was restored in the 1840s, Carl Leistler provided the furniture. Most chairs were like the one shown on the left, but in addition Michael Thonet manufactured chairs made out of palisander. The three models shown here, despite their different backs, are identical in their construction and consist of glued rod bundles bent three dimensionally.*

Carl Leistler, but he was persuaded to subcontract the job to the Thonets.

Thonet was now working in a court milieu and it was there, rather than in the homes and restaurants where it was later to prove so popular, that the Thonet chair was premiered and where contemporary critics noted that it stood in strange contrast to the more usual sumptuous, gilded court furniture. This was probably intentional, as at the time Thonet manufactured the Liechtenstein chairs as occasional furniture designed as flexible supplements to existing suites rather than pieces in their own right.

Although the work at the Palais Liechtenstein was completed by 1846, Thonet and his sons continued to produce chairs and parquet flooring for Leistler until, in 1849, Thonet suggested that he and Leistler go into partnership. He was to provide the patent and his and his sons' work, while Leistler would provide capital and the workshop. Leistler refused and it was this that gave Thonet and his sons the impetus to go into business on their own.

The first Austrian patent had expired on 16th July 1847, however - although a five year extension would have been possible - so from 1847 to the middle of 1852 Thonet worked as an independent manufacturer without the protection of a patent.

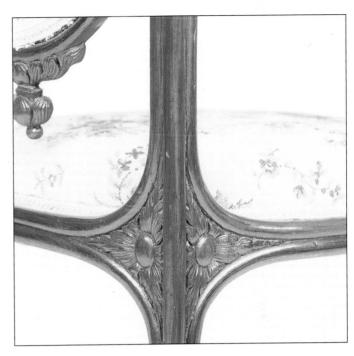

ABOVE: *The spaces between the U-shaped leg construction, the seat ring and the back rest were filled with carved wood.*

The Gumpendorf workshop

The Thonets had worked for other people for seven years, but now - with the continuing help of Desvignes - they were again able to set up their own workshop, at Hauptstraße 396 in Gumpendorf.

In the first year they created a chair which, although based on the Liechtenstein model, consisted of four pre-fabricated components which could be interchanged with parts from other models. This was the seed of Thonet's later model and type variations combined with mass-production. This chair no. 1 was probably part of an order for Count Schwarzenberg, who had commissioned light and elegant chairs for his garden palace from Thonet.

When Thonet designed a light chair that was also cheap, it was an instant success. He exhibited this model no. 4 at the Lower Austrian Craft Association in Vienna and the dainty chair caught the eye of the proprietress of the Café Daum, who wanted to transform her fashionable coffee-house from the Biedermeier style into a modern café with mirrors and light chairs. It was here that the chairs were on general view for the first time and soon afterwards Thonet received an order from Budapest for 400 of the light, flexible and sturdy 'Café Daum' chairs.

OPPOSITE: *These innovative chairs were also made by Thonet for the Palais Liechtenstein. The one on the right is made of polished palisander and has a continuous length of bent wood forming both the rear legs and the back. This became the hallmark of future series production. On the gilded chair, however, the back and seat are separate from the leg construction.*

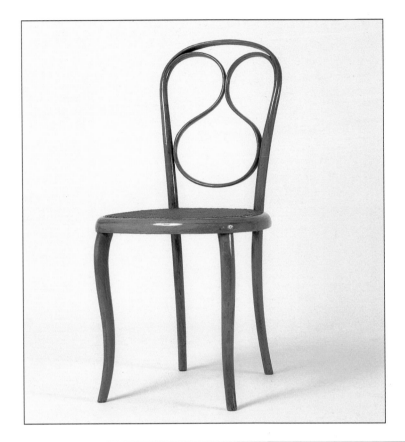

LEFT: *This is the earliest version of the so-called Schwarzenberg chair dating from 1850. Although it is constructed of laminated veneers, it already shows the most important characteristics of the later Thonet chairs.*

RIGHT: *The three Café Daum chairs show the transition from the early laminated veneer version of 1850/55 on the left, to the first solid bent wood version in the middle. The model on the right belongs to a series production after 1865 and consists of solid bent wood parts which are screwed together.*

ABOVE: *In London's Crystal Palace Michael Thonet's furniture was shown internationally for the first time at the 1851 Great Exhibition.*

The Great Exhibition

The Great Exhibition of 1851 - the first world fair - heralded the beginning of a new era marked by apparently unlimited faith in technology and industrialisation. This extended to furniture manufacturers, who now seemed capable of anything from a technical point of view and were faced with unlimited stylistic possibilities and a wealth of new markets. The exhibits Thonet sent to London's Crystal Palace were called a 'capriccio' - a curiosity - and they only won a bronze medal. In comparison with Leistler's sumptuous pieces, which took the gold medal, Thonet's work seems provocatively simple - although by his standards it was anything but. The items were made of beech wood covered with palisander veneer, tortoiseshell and brass; indeed, only the shape was truly characteristic of Thonet. Perhaps from the jury's perspective this faint hint of the style of industrial mass-production did make the pieces 'curiosities'. Desvignes, still Thonet's close friend and benefactor, bought all the exhibition pieces, which included a settee decorated with palisander veneers, two armchairs, six side chairs and a large round table inlaid with tortoiseshell, brass and mother-of-pearl. After Desvignes' death the pieces were returned to the Thonet family and then went to Bistritz.

The exhibition pieces also marked another important non-technical development for Thonet: the shift from single chairs to complete suites consisting of settee, armchair and chair. The 'Salon Garnitur' exhibited at Crystal Palace later became a series model: the settee as model no. 5 for three people, and the chair and armchair first as model no. 9, then as model no. 5.

MÖBEL
AUSGESTELLT AUF DER WELTAUSSTELLUNG LONDON 1851.

ABOVE: *The models made for the Great Exhibition were of palisander veneer on beech wood.*

RIGHT & DETAIL ABOVE: *The bent wood was inlaid with brass strips to accentuate the flow of the curves and give the furniture a sumptuous appearance.*

ABOVE: *The table tops of the furniture for the Great Exhibition seem like miniature versions of the parquet floors for the Palais Liechtenstein, but they were inlaid with tortoiseshell, brass and mother-of-pearl.*

RIGHT: *At the Great Exhibition Thonet showed, for the first time, his sets made of laminated veneer, the 'Salon Garnitur', which would prove so successful later on.*

As Thonet's products were now so successful, he probably applied for the second Austrian patent - which is dated 28 July 1852 - to stop the growing danger of reproductions. Two other companies producing laminated furniture - Josef Neyger and Johann Weiss - were also based in Gumpendorf and they simply copied Thonet. In detail their chairs did differ: the seat rings were solid wood, while Thonet used laminate strips, and they did not mark their furniture. It was only when Thonet started to bend solid wood that his competitors started to lag behind, as they had no money to invest in the appropriate tools. The technique described in the second patent is surprising because Thonet had used it for the last ten years - all the Liechtenstein chairs were produced in that way. Thonet applied for the new patent in the

name of his sons, although the company was not transferred to them for another 18 months.

Gebrüder Thonet

By the spring of 1853 the first workshop at Hauptstraße 396 had become too small and a new workshop was opened at Mollardgasse in Vienna. On November 1st 1853 the company Gebrüder Thonet (Thonet Brothers) was founded. Although Michael Thonet was only 57 and still very active, he transferred the business to his five sons who became co-owners - although he retained overall control and was the trustee for his youngest son Jakob, then only 12.

This decision to transfer the company to his sons so early allowed them to use their specific

ABOVE: *Michael Thonet and his sons from left to right: Michael jnr., Josef, Michael snr., August, Franz, Jakob.*

knowledge as businessmen, as well as craftsmen, to help the company gain international success and ensure the supremacy of the Austrian bent wood industry.

Under the name Gebrüder Thonet the company quickly achieved a world-wide reputation. For the 1854 Munich Industrial Fair they did not exhibit luxury items like those they had sent to the Great Exhibition, but sent 'consumer articles' instead: cheap, mass-produced pieces. It was the next year, at the 1855 Paris Exposition Universelle, that the great break-through to international markets was accomplished. Although the Press ridiculed all the Austrian exhibits, the Thonet pieces were highly acclaimed and were awarded a silver medal. Her Imperial Highness the Princess Mathilde bought up the entire Thonet stand and, more importantly, the first export contracts for South America were signed. This, however, brought its own unexpected problems: the glue of the laminated chairs dissolved in extreme humidity, so the wood began to split and lose its shape in the transport ships and the company was faced with a flood of complaints and the danger of losing the new market.

Thonet was again forced to re-think his wood bending technique and eventually decided that only the bending of solid wood would solve the problem. This was the last phase in the basic development of the bent wood technique.

Thonet also faced problems in Vienna around this time. With the increasing success of

Silver medal, Lower Austrian Crafts Association, 1862.

Gold medal, Altona, Germany, 1869.

Diploma of Excellence, Amsterdam, 1869.

Award certificate, International Exhibition, Sydney, 1879.

bent wood furniture, the difficulties with the Viennese cabinet makers' guild, which had begun in earnest after the foundation of Gebrüder Thonet, also increased. The guild wanted the second patent to be withdrawn as it was not innovative and the more successful Thonet became, the more he was ostracised. Although his competitors' complaints were heard sympathetically in the lower courts, the higher courts always found in Thonet's favour. Finally on July 8th 1855 Gebrüder Thonet received the authority to run a factory, freeing the company from the restraints of the guilds, which were only abolished in Austria in 1867.

ABOVE: *Medals and awards for Thonet furniture at international exhibitions and fairs.*

The patent for bending solid wood

Michael Thonet had already applied for a third patent in the name of his five sons. One month after he and his sons assumed Austrian citizenship on June 17th 1856, this third and most important privilege for industrial production 'to manufacture chairs and table legs of bent wood accomplished by steam or boiling liquids' was granted. The patent also mentioned the assistance of a metal strip secured to the wood by screw clamps - the key to the simple but brilliant technique that laid the foundations for the industrial mass-production of bent wood furniture. A year later the company also received authorisation to produce furniture, parquet flooring and other wood items. The competitors were now kept at bay, as none of them could prove that they had developed the solid wood bending technique. Ten years later, however, Jacob & Josef Kohn (Thonet's main competitors at the time) were so successful in attacking Thonet that Gebrüder Thonet voluntarily relinquished an extension of the third patent, which ran out in 1869.

The first factory: Koritschan

The demand for bent wood furniture soon outstripped the capacity of Thonet's second workshop in the Mollardgasse, although 70 people were working there and a specially constructed steam engine made production more efficient. Apart from the lack of space the company also had to contend with its increasing demand for beech wood - which had to be shipped to Vienna in barges along the Danube, making it expensive. Gebrüder Thonet therefore decided to transfer production from Vienna to the densely wooded areas of Moravia. In the little village of Koritschan 150 km north of Vienna they found all the prerequisites for the foundation of a factory: an abundance of beech wood, the railway and an unlimited reservoir of poor local workers. So, in the spring of 1856, Michael Thonet with his sons Michael and August moved to Koritschan. Franz, the oldest son, and Josef were left in charge of the Vienna company and the sales branch in the Palais Montenuovo - thereby already beginning the separation of production and marketing. As they had only a limited amount of capital, the Thonets not only drew up the plans for the factory themselves but also constructed all the necessary machinery - which must initially have been relatively crude and improvised, but nonetheless proved efficient enough at that stage.

Industrial furniture production

The concept of the Thonet factory was prototypical of entrepreneurial development in the 19th century: it had unlimited raw materials, cheap labour and good transport. The Austro-Hungarian Empire stood on the threshold of the transition from an agricultural to an industrial society, and so presented Michael Thonet with the ideal conditions for his enterprise. The beech wood forests, hitherto only used for fuel, were virtually untouched and the farming population, although freed from the constraints of feudalism, had neither land nor income and so provided an ideal labour force.

BELOW: *Bending forms incorporating a metal strip. On the left, the back for model no. 14, on the right, the back and arm rests for model no. 6009 and at the bottom, a foot ring.*

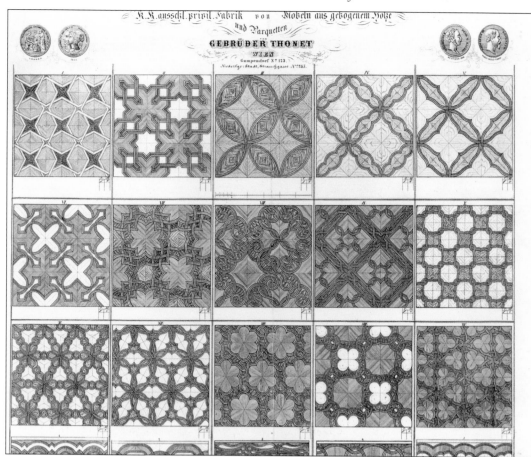

LEFT: *A selection of Thonet's intricate parquet floor designs made in the Gumpendorf workshop around 1842. The medals from left to right: London 1851, Munich 1854, Paris 1855.*

RIGHT: *Michael Thonet with his senior employees in Koritschan around 1860.*

33

It was in this environment that the new mass-production, with standardisation as its hallmark, was begun. From the first, the mass-production of Thonet furniture was based on the interchangeability of parts in different models. Initially the parts were still assembled in Vienna as the process was complicated, but the untrained local labourers soon learned how to produce complete pieces of furniture - especially, from the 1860s on, the chair no. 14, the 'consumer' or 'three florin' chair which had become both the main production article and the symbol of the company.

In May 1858 Thonet closed down the Vienna plant and all production was moved to Koritschan, although a new sales branch was opened in Vienna.

There was a precise division of labour within the new factory: men did the hard work, such as bending, sawing and steaming, while the women and the young helpers saw to the sanding, polishing and packing for half the wages. The weaving of the cane seats and backs was run as a cottage industry.

The work was hard and the hours long - 14-16 hours per day - and wages were low to keep prices to a minimum. Within management the division of labour was equally precise: Franz was responsible for export, Michael junior for Koritschan, August for the technical side and technique and Josef for the retail headquarters in Vienna. Jakob was still too young to be involved. At the end of his first decade of independent work, Michael Thonet was trying to reach all levels of buyer by offering a broad and varied range and being able to manufacture the cheapest mass-produced articles. Chair no. 14 eventually became the epitome of the cheap mass-produced consumer article and proved to be the foundation of the international success of bent wood furniture and the rise of Thonet.

ABOVE: *Illustration from the American catalogue of 1906/7.*

Further expansion: Bistritz and Nagyugrócz

Three years after Koritschan began production its capacity was no longer sufficient to meet demand, although 300 workers were producing 200 pieces of furniture per day. Indeed, demand had grown so much that there was now even a shortage of wood. To solve these problems it was decided to build a new factory in Bistritz, 50 km from Koritschan. Michael Thonet and his son August started there just as they had in Koritschan, taking great care to ensure that all the costs of the investment were met out of the company's profits to avoid any danger of repeating the Boppard experience - a principle the Thonets adhered to until the collapse of the Austro-Hungarian Empire. To train the new workforce, young people from Bistritz were sent to Koritschan, while experienced workers from the first factory went to work at Bistritz. After just one year production had reached 20,000 pieces per year - as much as the first factory - and the bulk of the production was still taken up with chair no. 14. Soon the two Moravian factories employed 800 workers between them and manufactured an average of 70,000 pieces of furniture each year. By 1865 total annual production had more than doubled to 150,000. The Thonet chair, the archetype of the modern consumer article, was suddenly in demand world-wide because of its low price, flexibility and durability. The market seemed inexhaustible and Thonet chairs were to be found in theatres, restaurants, sanatoria, hospitals, prisons, court rooms, public buildings, churches and other meeting places.

Just 10 years after the opening of the first factory, a third had become necessary. The need for raw materials determined the location and in 1865 a country seat with huge beech forests at Nagyugrócz in Hungary was purchased. This factory was initially conceived as a support for the other two, so that a sawmill and then a bending shop were built and half-finished

ABOVE: *All these models of the so-called 'consumer chair' date from around 1860. From left to right:*

Chair with laminated veneer back and a carved diagonally caned seat, manufacturer unknown.

Chair with laminated veneer back and a carved diagonally caned seat but with an additional foot ring, manufacturer unknown.

Version of model no. 8, with a seat ring of laminated wood, manufacturer Thonet.

A series model no. 8 from around 1870, the first version in solid bent wood, manufacturer Thonet.

LEFT: *The new Thonet factory in Bistritz.*

ABOVE: *Johann Strauss at the*
Vienna Hofball, 1865-70.

RIGHT: *Château Nagyugrócz in*
Hungary, where the Thonet
family built its third factory.

products were sent to Koritschan and Bistritz, but the ever-increasing demand for Thonet furniture throughout the world soon made it necessary to turn Nagyugrócz into a full production centre and the wood for the other two factories now had to come from Galicia, even further afield.

An autarkic empire

In line with the increase in production, the Thonet brothers acquired more and more land, so they now owned rather than leased everything they needed: the wood grew on their

land, the chairs were manufactured in their factories and sold in their international retail shops. In Wsetin in Moravia they even built a tool and hardware factory, so that they now made every last screw themselves.

In 1899 the first limestone factory to produce building materials for factories and houses was opened. The brickworks produced bricks with a Thonet stamp. Thonet now provided housing estates for the workers complete with schools, libraries, crèches and shops. Gebrüder Thonet had become an autarkic empire; however, the employees were completely dependent, even being forced to use Thonet's own currency.

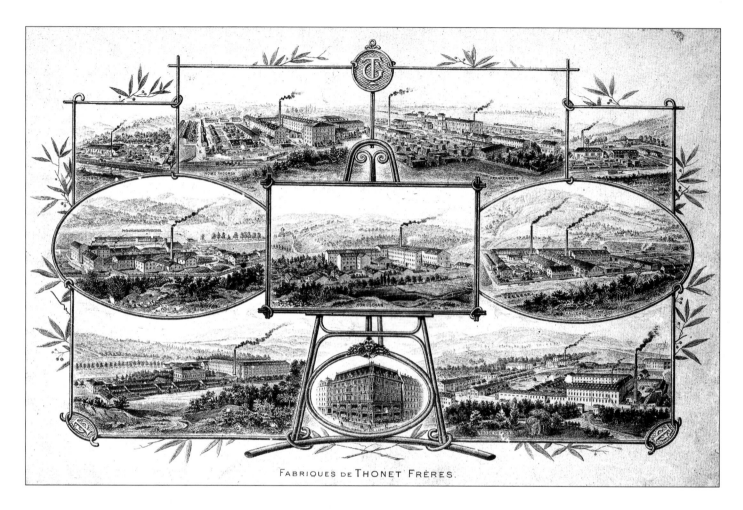

FABRIQUES DE THONET FRÈRES.

ABOVE: *The Gebrüder Thonet factories.*

Protective import taxes had just been introduced in some countries, which made those markets unprofitable, so to circumvent these duties new factories were also opened at Novo-Radomsk in Polish Russia and Frankenberg an der Eder in Germany.

Thonet's marketing strategy

The company's enormous success was also due in large part to the strict separation between production and marketing, which had begun when the first factory was opened in Koritschan. With the help of his sons, Michael Thonet had succeeded in developing an international marketing network that was well able to keep pace with the rapidly growing production. The extravagant retail branches, at the best addresses of all the major international business centres, were in themselves monuments to the legendary success of Thonet in the late 19th century.

The very first retail shop had been opened in Vienna in 1852, when the Thonets were still based in Gumpendorf. It was followed by a huge and sumptuous building in the prime Stephansplatz location. Thonet was also represented in major cities around the world: in the arcade next to the cathedral in Milan, in the Leipziger Straße in Berlin, in High Holborn in London, on the Boulevard Poissonnière in Paris and on Broadway in New York. There were also branches in Amsterdam, Brussels, Marseilles, Algiers, Moscow, St. Petersburg, Odessa, Chicago and all the major cities of the Habsburg Empire.

RIGHT: *The huge Thonet building on the Stephansplatz in Vienna, around the turn of the century.*

1859

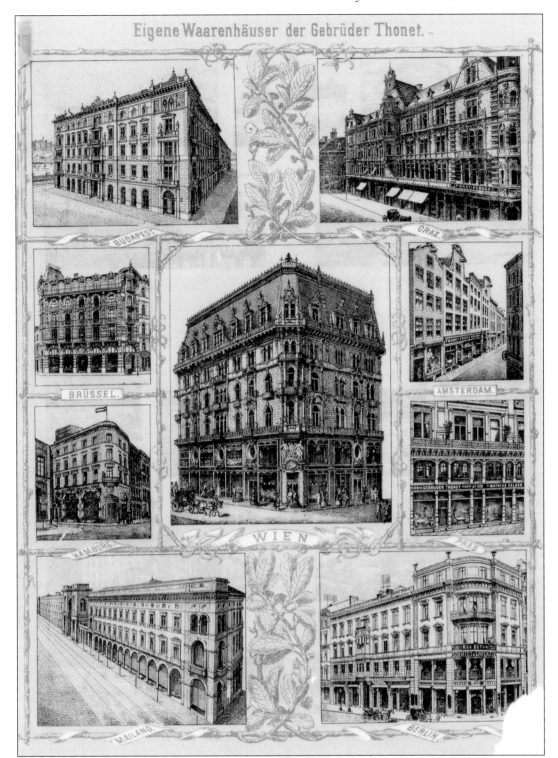

Eigene Waarenhäuser der Gebrüder Thonet.

Thonet's marketing strategy further hinged on the now famous multi-lingual catalogues, the first of which appeared around 1860 in the form of a poster listing all the models. It was deemed crucial that every model be shown and numbered, while later a carefully thought out ordering system was added, with the help of which it was easy to choose and specify the colour and type. These wide-ranging standard catalogues were later supplemented by specialised catalogues for theatres, restaurants, cafés, sanatoria and hospitals. The Thonet family's maxim to provide bent wood items for everyone and everywhere first becomes apparent in the 1885 catalogue: no place, no pursuit, no function was ever overlooked.

PAGES 42-45: *From chairs to tennis rackets, even as far as Africa: Thonet's production covered all areas of life anywhere in the world.*

RIGHT: *Bent wood chandelier by Thonet Bistritz around 1900.*

BELOW: *Armchair model no. 85 with desk, used by Emperor Franz Josef I of Austria. Thonet Vienna around 1900.*

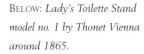

ABOVE: *Tennis racket, 1931.*

BELOW: *Lady's Toilette Stand model no. 1 by Thonet Vienna around 1865.*

LEFT: *Cameroon, 1907-12.*

LEFT: *Bed model no. 3 from Thonet Vienna 1883-84.*

EUROPE – 1900

■ = *Thonet factories*

SWEDEN

DENMARK

BALTIC
SEA

NORTH
SEA

• Copenhagen

• Danzig

• Hamburg

GREAT
BRITAIN

NETHERLANDS

• Warsaw

• Amsterdam

• Berlin

RUSSIAN
EMPIRE

GERMAN EMPIRE

BELGIUM

• Leipzig

• Breslau

■ *Novo-Radomsk*

• Cologne ■

• Brussels

Frankenberg

• Cracow

Galicia

Boppard ■

• Frankfurt

Ochotnica ■

Barwinek ■

LUX.

Prague •

Moravia

■ *Wsetin*

Bistritz ■■

• Paris

Koritschan ■

Hallenkau

■ *Nagyugrócz*

FRANCE

Munich •

Vienna •

• Salzburg

AUSTRO – HUNGARIAN

• Budapest

• Berne

SWITZERLAND

Zagreb •

Lyons •

• Milan

Venice •

EMPIRE

• Belgrade

Genoa •

SERBIA

• Marseilles

Sarajevo •

Sanjak of
Novibazar

MONTE-
NEGRO

SPAIN

*MEDITERRANEAN
SEA*

ITALY

*ADRIATIC
SEA*

• Rome

OTTOMAN
EMPIRE

BELOW AND RIGHT:
Convertible high chair, 1885.

As a result of sophisticated marketing techniques, by 1912 Thonet's production had reached its zenith with an output of 1.8 million pieces of furniture per year, two-thirds of which were chairs. The Austro-Hungarian Empire now absorbed only 15% of sales, while Russia, Germany, France and North and South America had become the most important markets.

ABOVE: *Thonet showroom in
St. Petersburg around the turn
of the century.*

LEFT: *Covers of Russian
catalogues – on the left, Thonet
and on the right, Kohn.*

ABOVE: *Emperor Franz Josef visits the Thonet factory in Bistritz in 1911.*

Thonet's competitors

Immediately after the last patent ran out in 1869 approximately 30 small bent wood companies sprang up in competition with Gebrüder Thonet, and by the turn of the century the market was limited because the number had risen to hundreds all around the world. Leopold Pilzer, who worked for the Austrian bankers Credit Anstalt, masterminded the consolidation of 16 of these smaller companies into one large bent wood company called Mundus AG. Pilzer was a shareholder in the new company, holding 6% of the shares. The market now had three main competitors: Gebrüder Thonet, Jacob & Josef Kohn and Mundus AG, all of whom banked with Credit Anstalt.

The onset of the First World War changed things drastically. Exports stopped, raw materials were in short supply and 75% of the workforce was conscripted. Thonet's factories were only able to work for two days a week and, as the Austro-Hungarian Empire had collapsed, except for Frankenberg they were now located in Poland and Czechoslovakia.

A price war had broken out between the three major manufacturers and this, in addition to the First World War, reduced profits so drastically that Kohn and Mundus merged in 1914. Gebrüder Thonet tried to hold out and continue as a family business, but in 1921 it became a joint stock company, Thonet AG, in order to sell shares. In 1923, however, Thonet was forced to merge with Kohn-Mundus to form 'Mundus-Allgemeine Handels-und Industrie-Gesellschaft', the largest furniture concern in the world. Leopold Pilzer was president with an 18% share in the new company. Gebrüder Thonet owned about half of the Mundus stock but only exerted influence over the former family business, which now consisted of independent national companies in Austria, Germany, and Czechoslovakia.

EUROPE – 1924

■ = *Thonet factories*

SWEDEN

LATVIA

BALTIC SEA

LITHUANIA

DENMARK • Copenhagen

FREE CITY OF DANZIG

NORTH SEA

Danzig • GERMANY

Hamburg •

GREAT BRITAIN

Amsterdam • NETHERLANDS

Warsaw •

Berlin •

GERMANY

POLAND

BELGIUM

• Brussels

Cologne •

Leipzig •

Brezlau •

■ *Noworadomsk (Novo-Radomsk)*

■ *Frankenberg*

LUX.

Boppard •

• Frankfurt

Saar

CZECHOSLOVAKIA

Prague •

Vsetin (Vsetin)

Cracow •

Ochotnica ■

■ *Barwinek*

• Paris

Bystřice pod Hostynem(Bistritz) ■■■ *Halenkov (Hallenkau)*

Koryčany (Koritschan) ■

FRANCE

Munich •

• Salzburg

Vienna •

Vel'ké Uherce (Nagyugrócz)

AUSTRIA

Budapest •

HUNGARY

ROUMANIA

• Berne

SWITZERLAND

Zagreb •

KINGDOM OF THE SERBS, CROATS AND SLOVENES

Lyons •

• Milan

Venice •

• Belgrade

Genoa •

Sarajevo •

• Marseilles

ITALY

SPAIN

MEDITERRANEAN SEA

• Rome

ADRIATIC SEA

ALBANIA

LEFT: *In 1931 Thonet-Mundus published a tubular steel catalogue which showed the colours on offer.*

As a result of the merger, the company soon reached 75% of pre-war production. The main clients were still hotels, cafés, restaurants and public buildings, but since the 1880s these had been joined by private households, for which the cheap, small and flexible furniture was ideal – especially in post-war years. At the end of the 1920s, the new architectural ideology equated tubular steel with modern living. Thonet-Mundus purchased the rights to the best furniture designs by leading architects and consequently led the field in tubular steel furniture from 1929 until the Second World War.

Mundus operated two separate companies in the USA - Thonet Brothers and Kohn-Mundus. In 1925 Thonet and Kohn-Mundus issued their first post-war catalogues, which were separate but identical. These American catalogues contained mostly period chairs rather than concentrating on the classic bent wood models, and tubular steel furniture was not offered as a stock item until 1933.

Towards the end of the 1920s Thonet Brothers opened a factory in Long Island, initially to assemble bent wood furniture made in Europe and to produce those items which were only sold in America. It also had an upholstery section to produce new designs in upholstered chairs and settees, although the mainstay of the American market were simple bent wood styles and period items.

ABOVE: *American catalogue covers from around 1930.*

LEFT: *The Düsseldorf Schauspielhaus (theatre) around 1935, with Thonet seats made of solid bent wood and plywood.*

The Second World War

Pilzer continued to purchase stock and when Credit Anstalt collapsed in 1931 he bought the Thonet-Mundus shares held by the bank, thus becoming the major shareholder. At this point the Nazis were coming into power in Germany and Pilzer, being Jewish, became concerned about the future. He moved the official headquarters of Thonet-Mundus to Switzerland and, in 1936, began the process of moving the company to the USA.

In 1938 Pilzer emigrated to the United States and sold the Eastern European and German factories back to the Thonet family, who in return relinquished its stake in Mundus Holdings. Gebrüder Thonet was allowed to manufacture for the markets east of the Rhine, while Thonet-Mundus - now based in the USA - kept the rights for America, France and England.

OPPOSITE: *In 1936, after extensive research, Hans and Wassili Luckhardt developed the prototype of the first Siesta Medizinal, a reclining chair that adjusts automatically to the movement of the body. Thonet produced the series from 1937.*

LEFT & ABOVE:
*American catalogue covers
from 1950 & 1955.*

A few key Thonet-Mundus executives also emigrated to America in 1939. Pilzer retained all rights to the Thonet name and trademark and formed Thonet Industries USA. He phased out the Kohn-Mundus name and purchased an old furniture factory in Statesville, North Carolina to manufacture bent wood furniture under the Thonet name. Many of the workforce for the new factory came from Europe and they speedily set about making the necessary machinery, tools and bending forms. The first Thonet bent wood chairs made in America left the Thonet factory in Statesville in 1941 and within five years the Statesville factory was producing 1,000 chairs per day. These chairs were made of elm, which had been selected as a substitute for the European beech.

The American company consisted of the Thonet Brothers factory on Long Island, with a showroom on Madison Avenue and the Kohn-Mundus showroom on Park Avenue. In France Thonet Frères was one of the smallest companies, but had its own factories. It was based in Paris and run by Pilzer's stepson Bruno Weill, who was an architect. Thonet Brothers Limited in London had offices and a showroom, but no manufacturing facilities.

Another American factory was opened in Sheboygan, Wisconsin in 1941, which was managed by another of Pilzer's stepsons, John L. Weill. These manufacturing facilities in the USA meant that business continued here despite the Second World War, while in Europe it came to an abrupt halt.

Post-war Thonet

After the Second World War it looked like the end of Thonet. The factories in Czechoslovakia, Poland and Hungary were nationalized by the Socialist governments. In Czechoslovakia Thonet became a state enterprise and in 1954 the company name was changed to Ton. Ton exported mainly to the Soviet Union. Thonet Industries, as legal successor to Mundus AG, later attempted in vain to claim the Czechoslovakian factories, and in the late

SUPPLEMENT 6103

SHOWROOMS: NEW YORK • CHICAGO • DETROIT
LOS ANGELES • SAN FRANCISCO • MIAMI • DALLAS
ATLANTA • STATESVILLE, N. C. • PARIS, FRANCE

THONET

THONET INDUSTRIES INC.,
ONE PARK AVE., NEW YORK 16, N. Y.
PHONE: MUrray Hill 3-1230
TELETYPE: N. Y. 1-1940

LEFT: *Supplement catalogue cover from 1961.*

BELOW: *American catalogue cover from 1955.*

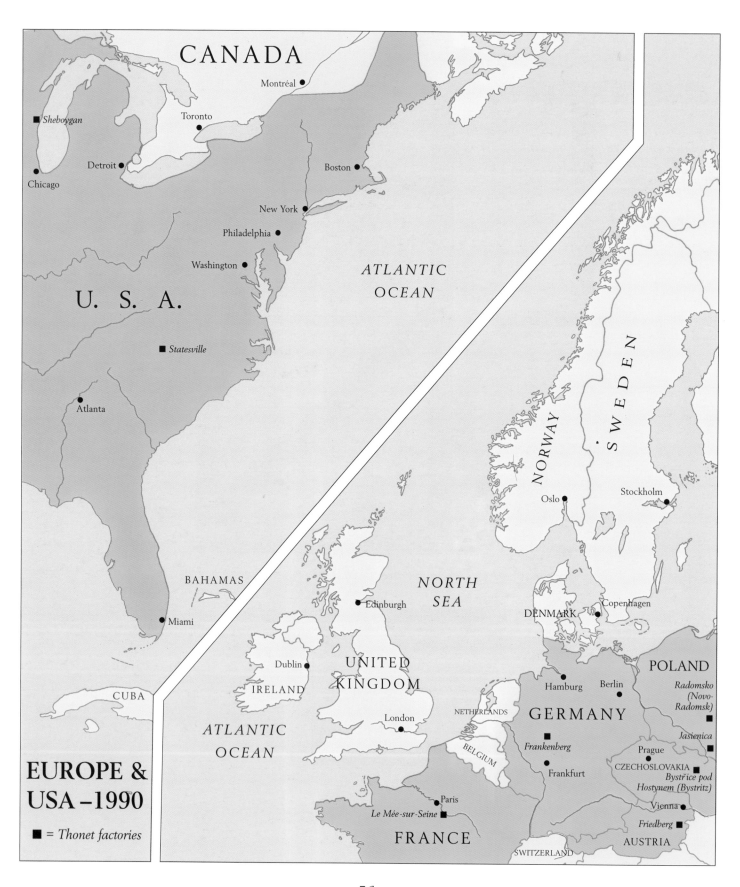

CANADA

Montréal ●

■ *Sheboygan*

Toronto

Detroit ●

Boston ●

Chicago ●

New York ●

Philadelphia ●

Washington ●

ATLANTIC
OCEAN

U. S. A.

■ *Statesville*

Atlanta ●

NORWAY

SWEDEN

Oslo ●

Stockholm ●

BAHAMAS

NORTH
SEA

Edinburgh ●

DENMARK

Copenhagen ●

Miami ●

Dublin ●

UNITED
KINGDOM

IRELAND

POLAND

*Radomsko
(Novo-
Radomsk)*

■

Hamburg ●

Berlin ●

CUBA

NETHERLANDS

London ●

GERMANY

ATLANTIC
OCEAN

Jasienica

■

BELGIUM

Prague ●

Frankenberg ■

CZECHOSLOVAKIA ■

Frankfurt ●

*Bystřice pod
Hostynem (Bystritz)*

EUROPE &
USA –1990

Paris ●

Vienna ●

Le Mée-sur-Seine ■

Friedberg ■

■ = *Thonet factories*

FRANCE

SWITZERLAND

AUSTRIA

1950s Pilzer himself filed a claim for the Polish factories and some restitution was made.

The Frankenberg factory in Germany had been completely destroyed by Allied bombers on the 12th March 1945; the Thonet House on Stephansplatz in Vienna had burned down and all the family property was lost. All that was left in Europe was the Thonet name. Georg Thonet - the great-grandson of the company's founder - began to rebuild the Frankenberg factory with the help of some former employees. Having put an emergency roof on the former recreation room, they produced their first post-war piece of furniture: a simple kitchen chair with a slat seat because there was no plywood. The old machinery was repaired as much as possible but production methods necessarily remained primitive. Slowly buildings were rebuilt and soon Thonet began again to manufacture bent wood chairs.

Five years later many of the former employees had returned, including those from the Bistritz factory. Their experience and knowledge was invaluable, as all the models and drawings had been destroyed.

In America Thonet Brothers Inc. had been least affected by the war and was looking to extend its market. Electronically moulded plywood seemed a commercially sound alternative to traditional labour-intensive bent wood, and indeed the technique was similar to that developed by Michael Thonet in the 19th century. Thonet Bentply, introduced in 1945 and proclaimed as 'solid-sturdy-strong-streamlined', proved so popular that Thonet could hardly keep up with demand.

The 1950s onwards

When the first Gebrüder Thonet post-war catalogue appeared in 1949 it featured many bent wood and a few tubular steel models from the 1930s. The tubular steel items were initially manufactured in rented space, but by 1950 they were again being manufactured in Frankenberg. New designs based on contemporary taste and demand were developed and in 1953 Gebrüder Thonet produced the first innovative post war model: chair no. 652 in wood and tubular steel. It was a great success and the profits from it were used to expand the Frankenberg factory. By 1955 the catalogues included plywood chairs, a large number of updated bent wood models and a new line of wooden chairs with upholstered seats and plywood backs. Similar models with thin tubular steel frames soon became very popular.

In 1951 Thonet Brothers Ltd in London was closed down by the American company and Thonet Frères in Paris became an autonomous company. In Austria Dr Fritz Jakob Thonet rebuilt Gebrüder Thonet AG Vienna, with the construction of a modern factory at Friedberg in 1963, which manufactured mainly rustic and school furniture; Thonet Vienna and Thonet Germany had been two separate companies since 1922.

In 1962 there were major developments in each of the far flung Thonet companies. Bruno Weill died and his brother, Hans, sold Thonet Frères to its manager, André Leclerc. The American company Thonet Brothers Inc. was sold to Simmons, a large bedding and hospital furniture manufacturer. Gebrüder Thonet in Germany agreed with the USA company that they would take over the rights to the Gebrüder Thonet trademark for Germany and the other countries of the European Economic Community. Several years later, in 1979, Simmons was sold to the Gulf & Western Corporation, and in 1985 the American Thonet Company, now called Thonet Industries, was taken over by successful businessman Manfred Steinfeld who, like Leopold Pilzer, had to leave Germany in 1938. Steinfeld owns Shelby Williams Industries, which manufactures inexpensive restaurant and hotel furniture.

In the 1960s there was a revival of bent wood and tubular steel furniture in both Europe and America and Thonet became a household name yet again. For example the classic model no. 14 was manufactured again, now known as model no. 214.

Throughout the following years Gebrüder Thonet in Germany continued to develop new models and continued to win awards. The greater output of Gebrüder Thonet, however, still consists of the classic bent wood models on which its original reputation was built.

The company Michael Thonet founded continues to faithfully represent the spirit of the age in which it finds itself, embracing new developments, both technical and stylistic. Michael Thonet's life work embodied the 19th century transition from the workshop to industrial mass-production. Half a century before Henry Ford he had already introduced division of labour as the basis for mass-production. He always used his material sensibly and cost effectively to achieve a result of style and stability.

Michael Thonet started as a modest cabinet maker, yet he envisioned and implemented production and marketing concepts which are now successfully used by multinational companies. Over a century later Gebrüder Thonet remains an enduring testament to its founder's vision of cheap, high quality, mass-produced furniture.

BELOW: *A bronze bust of Michael Thonet and,* OPPOSITE, *the Thonet family grave at the Vienna Zentralfriedhof.*

CHAPTER TWO

Wood Bending Techniques

Michael Thonet's experiments with making furniture by bending laminated veneers began in the 1830s. He had previously carved all shapes out of solid wood in the traditional manner, but this posed a considerable problem as it was impossible to carve curves entirely in the direction of the grain since it ran in a straight line. Where the curve began to go against the grain the wood became considerably weakened. Large curves were therefore traditionally constructed by gluing together many smaller curved pieces, each carved in the direction of the grain, a lengthy process incompatible with the ideas of mass-production.

Laminated veneer

Thonet therefore began to experiment with bending wood by cutting small pieces of veneer along the grain into strips of the same size. These were boiled in glue, several were then laid one on top of the other and finally they were bent into the desired shape in a mould. The moulds were initially made of wood, later of wrought iron and then of cast iron. The thinner the layers, the easier the part was to bend, so a greater number of thinner strips were required to mould more pronounced curves or to make stronger parts. The shapes which could be made by this method were therefore limited, but the construction elements which it produced were lighter, thinner and much stronger than conventional parts. In an attempt to achieve fast, cheap production, Thonet made his moulds as wide as possible so that he could then cut the laminates along their length once they had dried to produce several identical parts for his chairs. This laminated veneer technique is described in the 1st patent.

OPPOSITE: *Spiral, made out of one piece of bent wood and divided in the middle. It was made around 1880 to demonstrate the technical possibilities of bent wood at world fairs.*

BELOW: *A selection of iron wood-bending forms.*

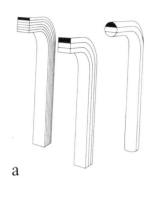

a

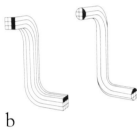

b

c

ABOVE: *Schematic drawings of the process of bending wood. After bending, the bundles were rasped and filed to give them a round cross section.*

a. Laminated veneer bundles bent in one plane.

b. Rod bundle bent in two planes.

c. Rods and narrow laminated veneer strips can also be bent axially.

Thonet tried three different methods of construction for the Liechtenstein chairs.

LEFT: *In the first, the back rest and the back legs form one unit.*

Laminated rod bundles

Thonet improved on his newly-developed technique when he began work at the Palais Liechtenstein by replacing the strips of veneer with thin squared rods which were boiled in glue, put together into oblong bundles and then bent. With these matchstick-like rods, Thonet was able to accomplish what had been impossible with the broad veneer strips: bending in two different planes. During the bending the rods slid against each other to form the curve, and stayed in place when the glue dried. As with the earlier method, the number of rods depended on the strength and curvature required, but Thonet generally used 64 rods in 8 x 8 bundles.

Thonet tried three different methods of construction for the Liechtenstein chairs. In the first, the back rest and the back legs are one unit, as in the later Thonet models. In the second, the bent rod bundles which form the back rest run round into the seat, so there is no direct continuation between the back rest and the back legs. To achieve the greatest stability and elasticity, Thonet glued four upside down 'U' shaped bundles of rods together in a square to form the four legs and a base for the seat. The third variety is a hybrid construction which uses both techniques. Thonet also changed the appearance of his work for the Palais Liechtenstein by rasping and filing the bent bundles until they had a round cross section.

The method 'to give the wood any desired curve or form in different directions by cutting or gluing it' is described in the second patent of 1852, but it has always been assumed that there was an interim stage where the laminated veneer strips were cut vertically into thin strips, then bent in another plane and glued back together. This is, however, probably incorrect, since the chairs for the Palais Liechtenstein were already being made of bundles of rods seven years before the second patent was registered.

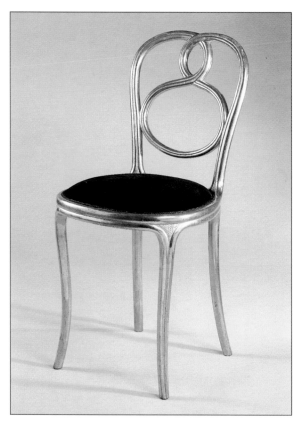

LEFT: *In the second, the bent rod bundles which form the back rest run round into the seat, so there is no direct continuation between the back rest and the back legs. The four legs and seat base are formed from four upside down 'U' shaped bundles of rods glued together in a square.*

LEFT: *The third variety is a hybrid construction which combines both techniques.*

Thonet continually altered and improved the bending process for rod bundles, according to the models. He either used 3 x 3 bundles of large rods (3 x 6mm) to form a strong inner core and covered them with four to five times as many very fine rods (1 x 1.5mm), or he formed the core from two solid wood strips (4 x 15mm) which were reinforced by thin rods (2 x 2mm) on the right and left, or at right angles with an additional strip (2 x 8mm).

Thonet was able to achieve the final perfection to his curves with the fine rod bundles by bending them axially. This had also been possible with the earlier veneer strips but it had severe economic drawbacks, because as soon as either veneers or bundles were bent axially, only one piece could be produced per mould. With the broad strips which were destined to be cut lengthways into several identical pieces, only the simplest bending in one plane could be done. The more complex the curves to be bent, the more preparation and work was required, and these conditions prevented Thonet from achieving his ideas of industrial mass-production.

The construction of the seat frame

The seat frames constructed in Boppard were made in the traditional way by gluing together four pieces of solid wood. It has always been assumed that even after working independently in Vienna, Thonet - like his Viennese competitors - continued to use this traditional method for the seats of his laminated models. Thonet, however, was already able to

LEFT: *An old wooden bending form used for seat rings.*

bend laminates in two planes, so he would have had no problem bending laminated strips in one plane to form seat rings. Thonet's perfectionism and his aesthetic preference for unity of form make it unlikely that he would have continued to use the primitive traditional method for his seat frames. Indeed, not a single traditional seat frame has yet been found bearing a Thonet stamp, although it is found on all laminated seat frames.

Thonet initially used a large number (8 -12) of very thin strips for his laminated seat rings. Strips which were too short could easily be lengthened with other strips without endangering the durability of the seat ring. The glued joint of the early seat rings was therefore staggered. From around 1860 Thonet began using three strong strips for his seat rings and securing the ends with glue and dowels.

The seat rings were initially trapezoid in shape and Thonet only began using round seat frames - made initially of three layers and later solid wood - when developing cheap products, especially chair no. 14. In later series production almost any shape of chair frame was made available.

Bending solid wood

It was only by the end of the 1850s, after using laminates for almost 25 years, that Thonet began bending solid beech rods. The motivation for this change came with the beginning of export to North and South America, because the furniture began to come apart during transportation by sea or on arrival as the hygroscopic glue absorbed moisture and lost its binding power. Thonet was faced with so many claims for damaged items that he had to find a solution quickly. He did so in 1856 when he managed to bend solid wood and was granted a patent - his third and last - 'to bend solid wood for chair and table legs'.

The problem with bending solid wood was that although the grain in the middle of the wood remains unchanged, forming a neutral layer, the surface layer on the inner curve is compressed while the surface layer on the outside of the curve has to stretch. If the wood is bent beyond its natural elasticity, this outer layer is inclined to split. Thonet solved this problem with a simple but brilliant idea: after watering and steaming the wood for a long time, a metal strip, roughly as wide and as long as the rod to be bent, was firmly attached to the rod with screw clamps at both ends. This strip was then kept on the outside of the curve during bending, so changing the normal physics of the process by not allowing the outside layer of wood to stretch. This, in effect, became the neutral layer and the rest of the wood was then compressed, which does not endanger the stability of the curve in the way that stretching does. With this development

ABOVE: *Thonet prevented the wood from splitting by attaching a metal strip to the bending form.*

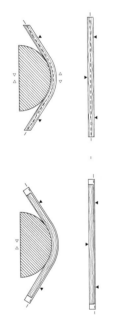

ABOVE: *When bending solid wood, the grain in the middle of the wood remains neutral, but the inner layer is compressed and the outer layer has to stretch. A metal strip attached on the outside of the curve changes the physics of the process by not allowing the outside layer of wood to stretch.*

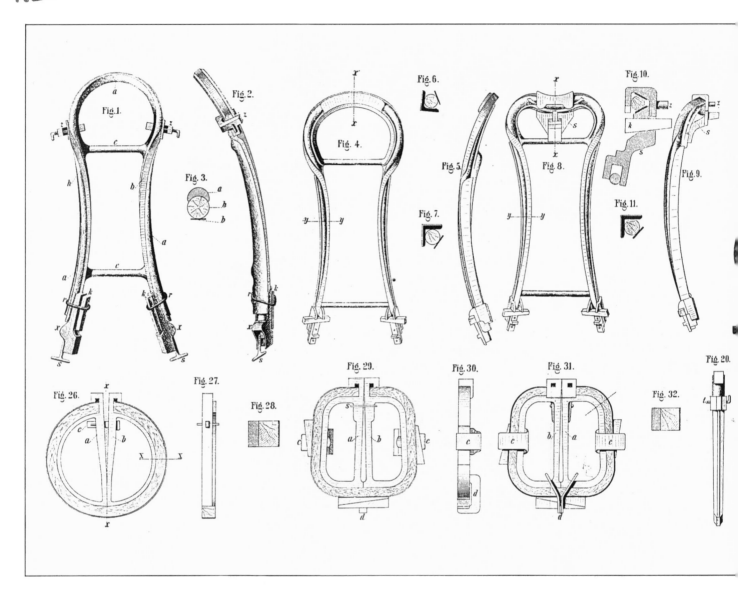

RIGHT: *A spiral made of solid bent wood. With items like this, Thonet demonstrated how easy it was to bend wood into any desirable shape.*

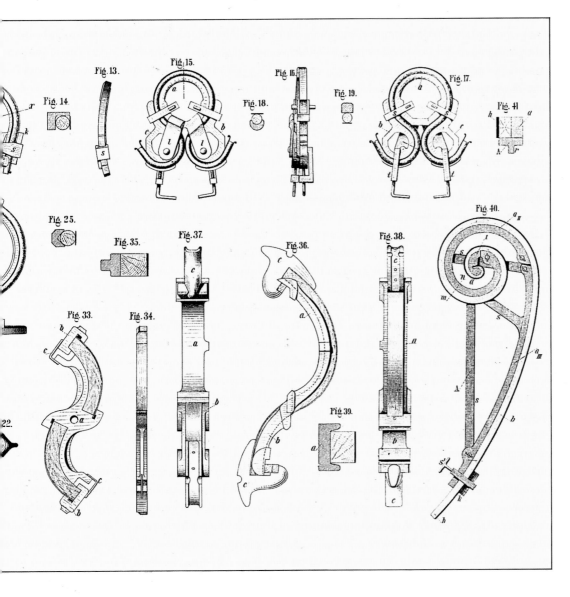

Thonet was able to circumvent the limitations of the natural qualities of wood and lay the foundations for the mass-production of bent wood furniture.

During the early years of solid wood bending, however, Thonet continued to use a variation on the old method for moulding tight garlands, whereby he cut the thin rods once or twice along their length up to the point where the strong curves began, coated them in glue and clamped them into the moulds. The early series models which were treated in this way do not suffer from the loss of curvature that can often be seen on tight curves bent purely of solid wood.

The industrial process of bending solid wood

The bent wood industry almost exclusively used the woods of the common beech for furniture manufacture. Although other hardwoods would also have been suitable, their bending strengths vary too much to make them suitable for mass-production. The selection of beech for the bending process quickly became very sophisticated; trees from the north faces of mountains and those from limy soil were preferred, especially if they reached the factory soon after felling.

ABOVE: *Beech logs are brought in from the nearby forests and sawn into boards by machine.*

RIGHT: *The beech wood boards are cut into rods of different lengths and widths to fit the various moulds. The rods are then put to soak in water for 24 hours.*

The process of manufacturing bent wood chairs in Bistritz around 1920.

ABOVE: *The rods are steamed at a pressure of 0.7 atmospheres and a temperature of 90-100°C.*

RIGHT: *Since they are now pliable, the rods are carefully bent in the wooden bending forms to achieve the desired shape.*

69

ABOVE: *Women sand and polish the chair parts.*

LEFT: *After drying in a special well-ventilated chamber at 60°C for a few days, the wood parts can be removed from the bending forms. The bent wood parts are then rasped and filed.*

RIGHT: *The seats and backs are hand caned by women.*

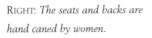

ABOVE: *Using templates, holes are drilled into the chairs before assembly.*

RIGHT: *Finally, the chairs are wrapped with paper and string and packed into crates to prepare them for transport.*

OPPOSITE: *The furniture which made both economic and design history is ready for delivery.*

CHAPTER THREE

From Biedermeier to Bauhaus

Michael Thonet's career began in the Biedermeier ('petty bourgeois' in German) era and the style was indeed bourgeois. It leant heavily on Europe's classical cultural inheritance, so that Thonet's work featured every kind of curve common in the art and architecture of antiquity including swinging volutes and carved rosettes.

As Thonet had not yet developed a method of bending wood in more than one plane his Boppard furniture, although revolutionary in construction, still looked a little stiff. The traditional construction of the seat frame and the use of woven cane - which was usual for Biedermeier furniture - further heightened the chairs' conventionality. Thonet, however, continued to use woven cane seats and what had once been characteristic of traditional Biedermeier furniture became a hallmark of Thonet as he grew ever more popular during the late Biedermeier period and beyond.

Thonet then developed another of his chairs' enduring motifs: the bent wood backrest incorporating a decorative loop that also helped strengthen the construction. The backrest became an independent and dominating form.

OPPOSITE: *Catalogue cover, Vienna, 1883.*

RIGHT: *The backrest of this Boppard chair features a decorative loop, which makes it look less stiff than the earlier models.*

ABOVE: *The backrest of the Café Daum chair. The elegant bent wood loop of the backrest became a hallmark of Thonet chairs.*

ABOVE: *Woven cane became a motif of Thonet furniture. Catalogue cover from around 1935 showing model no. A811/1F, designed by Josef Frank.*

OPPOSITE: *Armchair from a lavish suite manufactured for Count Palffy, which was made of laminated veneer and rods.*

The Rococo Revival

The Biedermeier style had, however, already given way to the Second Rococo in Vienna when Thonet arrived there and started working for Clemens List. List's work had been favourably mentioned as 'furniture in the Gothic style' in the catalogue of the 1835 Arts and Crafts Fair in Vienna and in 1839 he had caused a sensation with pieces in Chinese and Renaissance styles, which won a silver medal. It was through List that Thonet met Desvignes, who had been commissioned by Prince Alois Joseph II von Liechtenstein to restore his late 17th century city palace in Vienna.

With their work at the Palais Liechtenstein, the Thonets were able to prove their ability to the full - especially since the technique of bending wood lent itself ideally to the light curves of the Second Rococo. Although the Rococo Revival can be seen as the starting point for Thonet's chair models, he used the style in a simplified way.

The Court ambience

Although the Liechtenstein chairs were made for the sumptuous arena of the Court, they stood in contrast to the other magnificent furniture. They no longer belonged to the world of Biedermeier, where, typically, a settee and some chairs stood in a classical arrangement around a table, but were designed as occasional furniture.

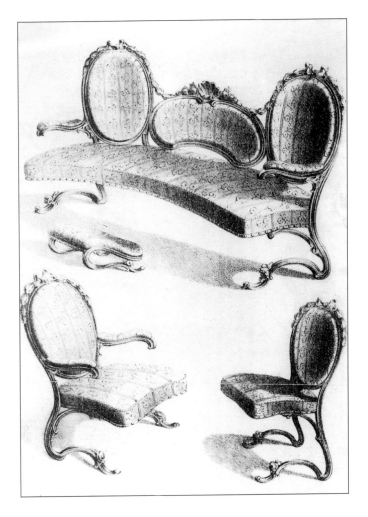

ABOVE: *Detail of the
'Sitzgarnitur' exhibits in
London's Crystal Palace,
showing the inlaid brass strips.*

ABOVE: *Design for a stylistically
as well as technically audacious
cantilever suite by Ferdinand
List, which was published
in 1851 in the 'Wiener
Möbel-Journal'.*

Thonet not only manufactured the light Liechtenstein chairs in the mid 19th century, but also produced more traditional and elaborate suites, such as the one made for Count Palffy, which consisted of a sofa, armchair and chair in the early floral decor style. These were developed, in a simplified form, into series models some 20 years later.

The first World Fair

The Great Exhibition in London's Crystal Palace gave furniture manufacturers a new esteem. Luxury was no longer the exclusive right of the aristocracy, but had become available to the increasingly large number of people with the money to afford it. It was this mentality, for example, which allowed the fashionable interior designer Ferdinand List to publish drawings in the Wiener Möbel-Journal of his designs for a suite that is stylistically and technically almost unsurpassable: a cantilever suite in laminated wood or cast iron. It was, in fact, only achieved three generations later and in tubular steel, but in the confident atmosphere of the time he would doubtless have found a clientèle interested in a drawing room suite on two legs in the Rococo style.

Leistler sent a complete suite to the Great Exhibition, including a luxurious library combination in the Gothic style which was later given as a personal present to Queen Victoria by the Austrian Emperor. It can now be seen in the Victoria and Albert Museum in London.

Thonet's pieces were regarded as comparatively simple, despite their technical virtuosity: they had been bent three dimensionally and brass strips 2-3 mm deep had been sunk between the rods to further enhance the elegant appearance of the curves.

The exhibition pieces included a settee of bent palisander veneers, two armchairs, six side chairs and a large round table inlaid with tortoiseshell, brass and mother-of-pearl. The shift from single chairs to complete suites of settee, armchair and chair was an important development for Thonet. The 'Salon Garnitur' exhibited at Crystal Palace later became a series model: the settee as model no. 5 for three people, and the chair and armchair first as model no. 9, then as model no. 5. Desvignes bought all the exhibition pieces, most of which are now in the Ton exhibition room in Bistritz.

ABOVE: *The chairs manufactured for the Great Exhibition in palisander veneer, which formed part of Thonet's 'Sitzgarnitur'.*

August Thonet and a new generation of bent wood furniture

August, the third of Michael Thonet's five sons and probably the most interesting, was technically extremely talented. The second generation of ambitious and innovative models is essentially attributable to him, of which the most extreme example is the Demonstration Chair,

RIGHT: *August Thonet (1829-1910), the talented engineer of the family, developed a number of innovative chair models.*

*The 'Demonstration Chair' by
August Thonet was shown
at every major exhibition
from 1867.*

which was first exhibited at the Paris Exposition Universelle in 1867. This was an experimental chair consisting of two round rods several metres long running in a continuous line, one forming the back and seat and the other the legs. The Demonstration Chair was supposed to be able to bear six tons according to the advertising, but this seems highly exaggerated. However, it served to demonstrate Thonet's technical skill and versatility.

OPPOSITE & RIGHT: *These experimental chairs from Bistritz were made out of solid wood, and not - as was often assumed - out of plywood.*

BELOW: *Brass model used to demonstrate how a chair could be cut and bent from a single plank of wood.*

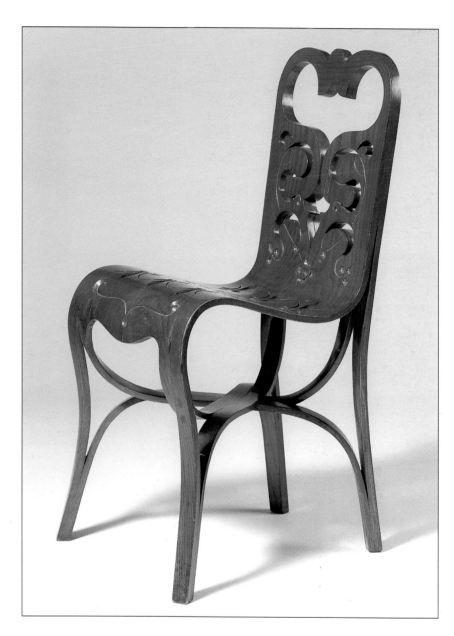

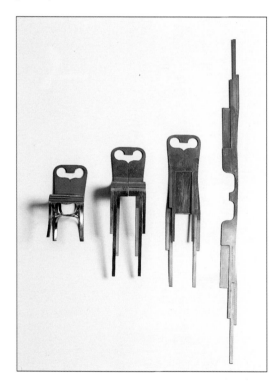

Interesting experiments were also undertaken in the prototype workshop under August Thonet's supervision. A beautiful example of a simple and logical chair was shown at the 1900 Exposition Universelle, but it proved too advanced for its time. In Bistritz the desire to cut a chair out of one sheet of material led to the bending of solid wood planks. Although the resulting items were technical masterpieces, they were stylistically more folk art than avant-garde.

Gebrüder Thonet created industrial products whose form followed logically from their construction technique, rather than placing the two in conflict. Building engineers had been the first to develop industrial production methods using prefabricated parts. Thonet applied the principles of steel construction to bent wood furniture manufacture – in both disciplines the goal was to achieve stability using as little material as possible. Bent wood furniture was regarded as 'unartistic', however, and unsuitable for a fashionable apartment, so for the home the furniture's industrial origins had to be concealed.

RIGHT: *During the Gründerzeit period, the taste for ornate pomp changed the look of bent wood furniture.*

Back to the Renaissance

As a commercial enterprise, Thonet did not concern itself with attempting to alter contemporary taste, but rather with providing what the market demanded. During the period of rapid industrial development and speculation known as the Gründerzeit, the lightness and modernity of Thonet furniture lay buried beneath heavy upholstery and richly carved ornamentation. On occasion, it even seems that during this period of historicism the aesthetics of light and delicate bent wood were completely submerged, with the addition of carvings and

ABOVE: *Thermoplastic designs for seats and back rests catered for all tastes.*

lathed front legs. Complex technical developments nonetheless took place simultaneously: in Nagyugrócz a thermoplastic veneer seat was developed. This allowed any pattern to be moulded into the seat, thus transferring different styles to the same basic furniture. Renaissance arabesques and Roman palmettes were popular, until they gave way to the lilies of Jugendstil around 1900.

The Gothic models, with their squared profiles, lathed legs, plywood seats and backrests of imprinted veneer, first appeared in the catalogue of 1885. These designs were not new, but

RIGHT: *The 1895 catalogue cover of Gebrüder Thonet Vienna, claiming that they are the sole inventors of bent wood furniture and the founders of the industry.*

redecorations of existing models; indeed, Thonet now manufactured a number of bent wood chairs in the prevailing historicist style, as part of his attempt to reach as broad a market as possible. By 1888, nine different types of chairs, two rocking chairs and thirteen salon models were produced with the fashionable squared profile which had been introduced by J & J Kohn at the Philadelphia world fair. The Thonets followed the stylistic preference of the unstoppable bourgeoisie as they rose to prominence during the Gründerzeit and aimed to fill their houses with furniture from the new department stores, where 'style' could now be bought. Thonet's easel was very much in demand to hold the hemp prints imitating oil paintings, which were then all the rage. Originals were no longer in demand because industry offered everything conceivable by catalogue. In this sense the Thonet publicity material and catalogues constitute a vivid testimony to the age and its bourgeois inclinations.

Thonet and the Jugendstil

Characteristically Thonet did not remain unaffected by the Jugendstil (the German manifestation of Art Nouveau); indeed, it proudly announced in its 130 page catalogue of 1904 that its new series model no. 221 had already sold by the millions. It was not only the shapes and motifs of bent wood furniture that changed with the onset of the Jugendstil, but also its appreciation. Whereas it had previously been purely a consumer article, it now entered the realm of art and was lifted from anonymity into the awareness of an elite which was increasingly interested in contemporary style.

OPPOSITE & RIGHT: *The Jugendstil, with its decorative motifs, dominated Thonet's chairs and settees for many years.*

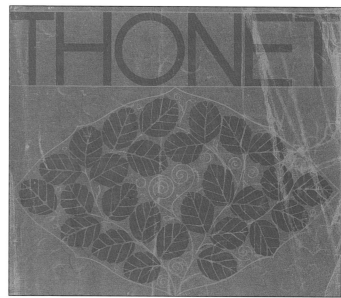

OPPOSITE: *Cover of the 1910/11 catalogue of veranda suites, mostly designed by Vienna architect Marcel Kammerer.*

ABOVE: *Catalogue cover from around 1910, in the Jugendstil of the period.*

ABOVE: *Catalogue cover from Vienna, 1911.*

Architects also began to take an interest in bent wood. When the Viennese architect Adolf Loos modernised the Café Museum in 1899, he used traditional bent wood furniture. This was the first time an ordinary industrial product was linked to a well-known creative architect. Loos worked with an oval instead of a circular cross section for the wood in his chairs, to create a purely functional object. The foundations of Adolf Loos' conception of bent wood were: 'what is useful is beautiful'.

Bent wood furniture design was swept by the fashion for making 'art' out of every last consumer article, from which the Jugendstil grew. It was not Thonet itself but its strongest competitor, J & J Kohn, which led the way in this attempt to combine industry with art, and specialists in this field - the 'art-architects' - were now employed. The achievements of the art-architects were described by Ludwig Hevesi in 1901: 'The Thonet chairs had conquered the world and then they ossified. They remained confined to restaurants and concert halls. Now the art-architect has given bent wood a new meaning... Now it has a new future.'

Even the fact that Kohn used squared rods opened up numerous new markets, because it transformed bent wood furniture into an ambitious contemporary genre. In its new squared shape, bent wood became a stylistic novelty and rose from the utilitarian sphere of offices and cafés to art-salons, where it won the highest acclaim. Bent wood had become chic.

There was now no longer any ideological difference between Otto Wagner's school of architects, the Sezession (Vienna Secession), founded in 1897, the Wiener Werkstätte (Vienna Workshop), founded in 1903 and the new bent wood furniture. The boundaries between free and applied art had been completely broken down in this area, and a new and important furniture genre was born: the architect-designed Viennese bent wood furniture in the Secession style.

OPPOSITE: *The big
cashier's hall of the Vienna
Postsparkasse, which made
design history.*

BELOW LEFT: *The 'seating
machine' by Josef Hoffmann,
from around 1905, has become
the epitome of the Vienna
architect style.*

BELOW RIGHT: *The stool
designed by Otto Wagner for
the Postsparkasse was later
offered by Thonet as series
model No. 4746.*

The 'Postsparkassen' style

The prototype of the new generation of bent wood furniture was a chair by Gustav Siegel, which had already won several medals at the 1900 Paris Exposition Universelle. It was originally produced by Kohn, but Thonet copied the concept.

In 1902 the Viennese architect Otto Wagner designed a similar chair for the telegraph office of 'Die Zeit' and in 1904 he began work on the famous Postsparkasse in Vienna (the Vienna Postal Savings Bank), which was to become a milestone of modern architecture. Assisted by Marcel Kammerer, he designed several bent wood models for the project, including an armchair and stool, a desk and book shelf. When the Postsparkasse was expanded in 1912 anonymous Thonet chairs were used with a simple varnished finish, in accordance with Wagner's insistence that what was not useful could not be beautiful. Wagner also thought that developments in style should come about as a result of new construction techniques and materials, and that these offered such a wealth of opportunity that it would no longer be necessary to imitate old styles, as had previously been the practice.

Josef Hoffmann is famous for several style-setting designs in bent wood for Kohn, including the dining chairs for the Purkersdorf Sanatorium around 1905 and, in the same year, the chairs for the 'Cabaret Fledermaus', which served Thonet and Kohn as a prototype. Hoffmann's 'seating machine' from 1905 is the epitome of the Vienna architect style. The determination of style by function, which marked the style of the Vienna Workshop in the 1920s, became typical of the Art Deco.

When Hoffmann created the Kohn Room for the 1914 Cologne Werkbundausstellung, however, he changed from this functional style to an Empire character in his work. In the catalogue of 1904 Thonet offered a greater type variation, but had not fundamentally changed its style: classic and historicist models are found side by side with Art Nouveau models based on the English Windsor chair and, from 1911, the Morris chair.

Nr. 1511   Nr. 511

LEFT & BELOW: *This arrangement with chair model No. 511 is shown in a Thonet Jugendstil catalogue. Chair 511 has elements of the French Art Nouveau and the Vienna architect style.*

RIGHT: *This table by Marcel Kammerer was manufactured by Thonet in squared profile beech wood and stained mahogany red.*

BELOW: *Catalogue of furniture for bathrooms and hospitals, from around 1914.*

Those models which were specially designed for Thonet by architects are only to be found in the supplementary catalogues from 1911-1915. The Thonet models which had been designed by Otto Wagner's colleagues, or in the stylistic environment of the Postsparkasse, appeared first in 1905 in 'Das Interieur' and only later in Thonet's supplementary catalogues, in which variants of the Siegel chair and many others were also to be found.

The Vienna architects

The furniture for the Thonet Pavilion at the 1913 International Construction Industry Exhibition in Leipzig was designed by Otto Prutscher and has a number of playful details. He

BELOW: *Catalogue No. 31, which was issued by Gebrüder Thonet AG of Frankenberg in Germany, in 1931.*

also designed the furniture for the 1914 Werkbund exhibition in Cologne, which already demonstrated the Art Deco tendencies of the late Vienna Jugendstil furniture.

In Thonet's catalogues no attempt was made to differentiate the company designs from those by the architects, which were placed next to each other. Although the designs for bent wood furniture were often the work of renowned architects such as Adolf Schneck, Josef Frank, Ferdinand Kramer and Josef Hoffmann, their names were not used to attract clients, as became usual with the later tubular steel designs. In accordance with the old Thonet tradition, the client should only associate new bent wood furniture models with the established name of quality: Thonet.

It was not only the low price that helped to revive interest in Thonet furniture after the First World War; a new generation of architects also saw an important precedent for their ideological and social demands in the timeless, unpretentious, mass-produced items of Thonet.

In the 1920s, exhibitions like the Exposition des Arts Décoratifs in Paris in 1925 - including a pavilion by Le Corbusier - and the Werkbund exhibition at the Weißenhof Siedlung in Stuttgart in 1927 – under the German architect Mies van der Rohe – demonstrated the contemporary state of bent wood furniture. The designs were neither new, nor the products of the architects; nonetheless, their timeless quality demonstrated their industrial origins.

Despite this new state of affairs, Thonet-Mundus launched an international competition in 1929 to try to find a contemporary 'key model', which would lead the way for the future of seating much as the Thonet chair no. 14 had earlier. The jury included famous architects and designers like Le Corbusier, Pierre Jeanneret, Gerrit Rietveld, Adolf Schneck, Bruno Paul and Gustav Siegel, who examined over 4,000 entries but were unable to find an outstanding design. 'The Vienna chair festival is definitely over,' commented the Frankfurt architect Ferdinand Kramer.

CHAPTER FOUR

From Bent Wood to Tubular Steel

Thonet's association with tubular steel dates from the end of the 1920s, when, as Thonet-Mundus, the company began to propagate the new architectural ideology which equated tubular steel with the idea of modern living. It was a logical consequence for the bent wood industry to switch to tubular steel. Thonet purchased the rights to the best designs by leading architects and consequently led the field from 1929 until the Second World War.

The avant-garde architects

Half of Thonet's production in the early 1930s was designed by Marcel Breuer, who was equally at home with both utilitarian and elegant models. Unusually, however, Thonet purchased the best designs not only in Germany but also in France, where an independent tubular steel tradition had grown up under Le Corbusier. The co-operation between German and French manufacture was unique for the time and was only possible because of the international nature of the Thonet-Mundus company.

After Leopold Pilzer bought Thonet-Mundus stock, his stepson Bruno Weill, who was

LEFT: *Multilingual cover of the Thonet export catalogue from 1938.*

OPPOSITE: *Modern production model of the Mies van der Rohe cantilever chair.*

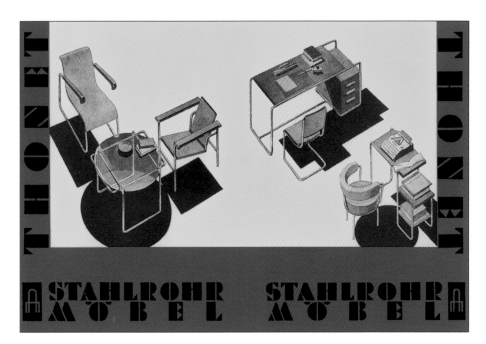

B 3
Thonet

ABOVE: *Thonet's 1930-31 tubular steel catalogue, which consisted of loose cards in a folder.*

ABOVE RIGHT: *In the 1960s, the Italian furniture manufacturer Gavina named the famous model no. B3 chair - designed by Marcel Breuer in 1925 - the 'Wassily' after Breuer's colleague at the Bauhaus, Wassily Kandinsky.*

an architect, took over the management of Thonet Frères in France. Weill was extremely progressive and not only mass-produced his own designs - which were marked 'Béwé' - but also those of the team of Le Corbusier, Charlotte Perriand and Pierre Jeanneret (who were regarded as very avant-garde), Lurçat and the architects Guillot and Guyot.

The first large catalogue of 1930-31 consisted of a folder of 50 cards and combined a German contribution, in the shape of Marcel Breuer's most important designs, with the best of the corresponding French models.

The cantilever chair

The work of Marcel Breuer - a teacher at the Dessau Bauhaus - was crucial in the development of tubular steel. He produced many influential designs between 1925 and 1927, and was the most intelligent and consistent in the realization of the Bauhaus ideas – as is shown by his world famous chair model B3. He also developed a double cantilever chair, which was exhibited at the Deutsche Werkbund section of the Salon des Artistes Décorateurs in Paris in 1930. His inspiration, as well as that of Mies van der Rohe who was one of the 20th century's most important architects, came from the Dutch architect Mart Stam. Stam must have shown his colleagues a sketch of his new chair during the preparation for the Werkbund exhibition at the Weißenhof Siedlung in Stuttgart in 1927. Stam was obsessed by the idea of a cantilever chair, as were his colleagues, who wanted to apply the principle in architecture as well as furniture.

Ludwig Mies van der Rohe immediately started work on his own design for a cantilever chair and he was granted a patent three days before the Weißenhof Siedlung exhibition opened. What Mies van der Rohe wanted to protect before he showed his chair was not the shape, but the principle of the suspension.

It was more difficult for Breuer because he never managed to separate his own cantilever chair designs from Mart Stam's idea - not least because Breuer originally worked for Standard Möbel, whose manager Anton Lorenz had acquired the usufruct (right to manufacture the design) from Stam.

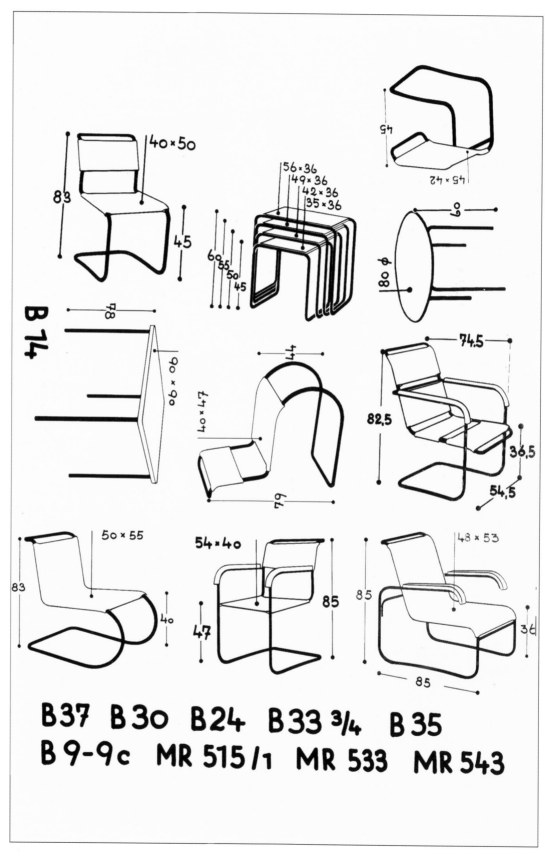

RIGHT: *Illustration from the 1932 Thonet catalogue, in which the company introduced schematic drawings indicating dimensions.*

RIGHT: *Marcel Breuer's double cantilever chair on runners stood in the cafeteria of the Gropius Pavilion at the 1930 exhibition of the Société des Artistes Décorateurs in Paris.*

MIËS VAN DER ROHE LE CORBUSIER BREUER LURCAT BÉWÉ

MODERNE STALEN MEUBELEN

THONET
KEIZERSGRACHT 213
AMSTERDAM-C.

RIGHT: *A leaf from Thonet's tubular steel furniture catalogue in Holland in the early 1930s.*

OPPOSITE: *Thonet catalogue cover 'Small Furniture' from around 1935.*

The Lorenz monopoly

Standard Möbel was taken over by Thonet-Mundus in 1929. Thonet believed it had purchased the rights to Stam's cantilever chair along with Standard Möbel, but Lorenz successfully argued in court that while Thonet-Mundus had bought the company, he personally still enjoyed the rights to the chair.

Lorenz then founded the DESTA Company, which, three years later, was also taken over by Thonet, but he still received royalties for his cantilever patents from Thonet because, again, he had registered all rights in his own name.

This 'Lorenz Monopoly' provoked interesting reactions from other designers forced to find variations which could not be attacked on the basis of the Lorenz/Stam patent. It was as a result of this pressure, for example, that Marcel Breuer improved on the original idea with the principle of a chair on runners (model B35) with a free-swinging seat - the first double cantilever chair - probably using the Mart Stam chair as a prototype. This was one of the great tubular steel designs of its time and is still manufactured by Thonet today. The Lorenz monopoly may also have given rise to another Thonet cantilever chair, model B257, which was developed in France by Guyot.

The bourgeois revival

The 1932 Thonet catalogue introduces the designs of Mies van der Rohe and Lilly Reich from the late 1920s - although Lilly Reich is not mentioned as a designer, the LR being changed into MR. Mies van der Rohe, the last great designer not working for Thonet after Le Corbusier and Breuer had joined the company, finally signed a contract with Thonet in November 1931. Thonet now also began to manufacture the Mies van der Rohe cantilever chair as model MR 533. The sale of Mies van der Rohe models alone brought in 600,000 Reichsmark in 1937.

In that year's catalogue, however, it became clear that popular tastes could not be changed as radically as the architects had hoped at the end of the 1920s. The strict architectural designs sat oddly with the more popular pieces, which included small items, upholstered chairs, dressers, flower and umbrella stands. During the 1930s tubular steel moved away from the avant-garde towards bourgeois conformism - even the room displays of the 1932 catalogue

reflected the bourgeois taste with glass cabinets full of bric-à-brac. The days when Thonet had dared to present tubular steel as pure and abstract had passed. It was perhaps symptomatic that Breuer's B3 chair, the symbol of avant-garde later named the 'Wassily', was now nowhere to be found in the catalogue and it was not re-introduced until the 1960s.

The real success of tubular steel furniture showed itself only 30 years later, in the 1960s, when the Bauhaus models became classics, took the place of model 14 and were produced by the million.

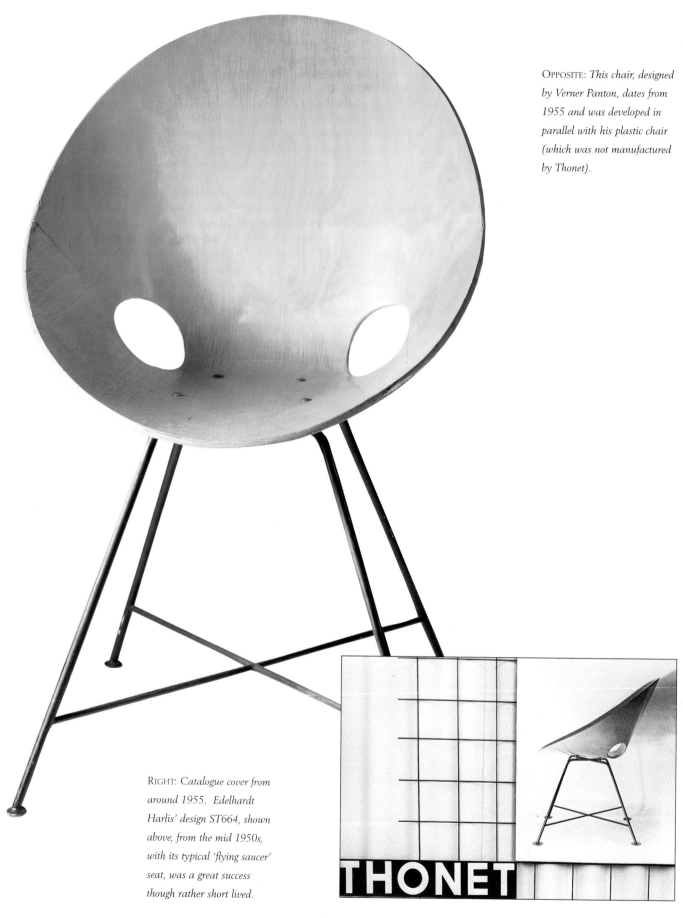

OPPOSITE: *This chair, designed by Verner Panton, dates from 1955 and was developed in parallel with his plastic chair (which was not manufactured by Thonet).*

RIGHT: *Catalogue cover from around 1955. Edelhardt Harlis' design ST664, shown above, from the mid 1950s, with its typical 'flying saucer' seat, was a great success though rather short lived.*

THONET

RIGHT: *The Flex chair, designed by Gerd Lange in 1973-74. It was part of a commercial, stackable seating system which could be adapted with different arm and leg attachments.*

By the mid 1930s the political and artistic landscape of Germany had changed and under Hitler no compromises were possible. By 1935 the Bauhaus had already ceased to exist as an institution for two years and some leading designers were working in Switzerland and England, from where they would eventually emigrate to the United States. The catalogue of 1935 reflects this change. Although the most important models of the Dessau Bauhaus are still included, they are integrated in a non-committal way. The daring élan of the early architectural style had given way before the onslaught of the conformist lifestyle of Mr. Average.

When the first post-war catalogue appeared in 1949 it featured many bent wood and a few tubular steel models of the 1930s, but in 1953 Gebrüder Thonet produced the first innovative post-war model. Chair no. ST 664 was designed by Edelhardt Harlis with a conical plywood seat and iron rod legs. It was such a success that the profits from it largely financed the expansion of the Frankenberg factory. By 1955 Gebrüder Thonet offered plywood chairs, a large number of updated bent wood models, a new line of wooden chairs with upholstered seats and plywood backs, and models with thin tubular steel frames.

The company continued to grow and develop new chair designs and in 1974 the Flex chair, designed by Gerd Lange, was introduced. Its basic form consisted of a moulded plastic seat and four stout round wooden legs, but it could be adapted with different arm and leg attachments. It was designed as a commercial seating system and was extremely lightweight and adaptable.

RIGHT:
The Breuer cantilever chair was based on Stam's principle, but introduced a fixed frame system for the back and seat. It is still manufactured by Thonet today as model no. S64.

CHAPTER FIVE

Vintage Models

Although originally a product of their era, Thonet chairs have survived the passing of time. Indeed, their design is now prized more highly than ever, with many models regarded as contemporary classics.

Michael Thonet was not only an industrial pioneer, but also produced some of the most beautiful and enduring chair designs of the 19th century. Model no. 14, for example, a pre-Industrial Revolution design which was perhaps the most popular chair in the world in the 19th century, is still fashionable today and is manufactured in great numbers. The appeal of the Thonet chair stretched from the Court, through commercial milieus such as cafés and offices, to the home.

Michael Thonet combined a very high standard of design with modern techniques of mass-production in a way that was unique at the time, and his ideas, as well as his manufacturing methods, were widely copied. The company he founded remained at the forefront of contemporary design, and movements such as the Jugendstil, the Vienna Architects and the Bauhaus had a great impact on the style of Thonet furniture.

Although bent wood has become unfashionable several times since Michael Thonet first started production, it has also been rediscovered more than once this century and has certainly proved its resilience. Perhaps its most unexpected champions were the avant-garde designers. As Le Corbusier put it: 'We have introduced in the Pavillon de l'Esprit Nouveau, as we have in our mansions and in our modest working class houses, the humble, bent wood Thonet chair....And we believe that this chair, millions of which are in use in our continent and the two Americas, is a noble thing, for its simplicity is a distillation of the forms that harmonize with the human body.'

By the end of the 19th century, the name of Thonet had become a synonym for bent wood and its use in industrial furniture production world wide. When tubular steel furniture was introduced, however, the Thonet company quickly moved into the new field and soon began to set the tone internationally. Although not known as the inventor of tubular steel furniture, Thonet-Mundus bought and manufactured the best designs. Many of these chairs, such as Marcel Breuer's models B35 and B32, were re-edited by Thonet Frankenberg and are still manufactured today.

Thonet chairs made design history and some of the models - in both bent wood and tubular steel - have, through their beauty, their functional form and their enduring appeal, become design icons.

OPPOSITE:

Catalogue cover, Vienna 1885.

The Boppard Chair (c.1836)

The Boppard chair represents Thonet's first experiments with bending laminated veneers. Aesthetically the Boppard chair still belongs to the Biedermeier, but its construction principle was innovative because the two sides were built with laminated veneers, which made it lighter and cheaper than a conventional chair. The seat frame, however, was still carved and joined in the traditional manner and the bent parts were covered in veneer to hide the construction. Michael Thonet used this first version, shown opposite, to demonstrate his technique of bending laminated veneers when he first applied for a patent.

The Boppard chair shown on this page is a more elaborate version, in which the wood of the back rest links the two sides.

111

The Liechtenstein Chair (1843)

The earliest chairs for the Palais Liechtenstein, which date from about 1843, formed a sort of prototype for the later series models. They demonstrate Thonet's most important achievement: the three dimensional bent curves that were made possible by using bundles of very fine rods.

There are three types of Liechtenstein chair, which vary according to their construction: on the first the back rest and the back legs are one unit; on the second type the back rest runs into the seat, so there is no direct continuation with the back legs; the third variety is a hybrid construction using both techniques. The design where the back rest and the back legs were bent from a single piece proved extremely successful in the later Thonet chairs. This important development, which can be regarded as the technical turning point in the development of the Thonet chair, doubtless owed much to Desvignes' influence. The only changes needed to adapt the chair for mass-production were the positioning of the front legs and the use of solid wood instead of bundles of thin rods.

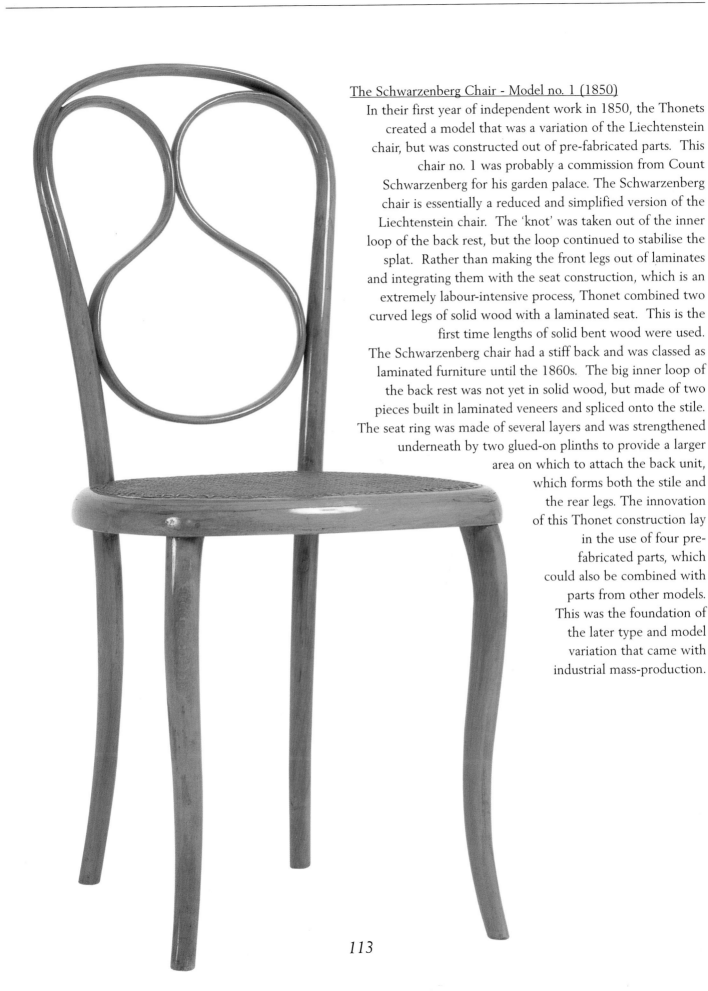

The Schwarzenberg Chair - Model no. 1 (1850)

In their first year of independent work in 1850, the Thonets created a model that was a variation of the Liechtenstein chair, but was constructed out of pre-fabricated parts. This chair no. 1 was probably a commission from Count Schwarzenberg for his garden palace. The Schwarzenberg chair is essentially a reduced and simplified version of the Liechtenstein chair. The 'knot' was taken out of the inner loop of the back rest, but the loop continued to stabilise the splat. Rather than making the front legs out of laminates and integrating them with the seat construction, which is an extremely labour-intensive process, Thonet combined two curved legs of solid wood with a laminated seat. This is the first time lengths of solid bent wood were used. The Schwarzenberg chair had a stiff back and was classed as laminated furniture until the 1860s. The big inner loop of the back rest was not yet in solid wood, but made of two pieces built in laminated veneers and spliced onto the stile. The seat ring was made of several layers and was strengthened underneath by two glued-on plinths to provide a larger area on which to attach the back unit, which forms both the stile and the rear legs. The innovation of this Thonet construction lay in the use of four pre-fabricated parts, which could also be combined with parts from other models. This was the foundation of the later type and model variation that came with industrial mass-production.

Above: *Early Café Daum chair, made of laminated wood veneer strips.*

Left: *French garden chair in wrought iron, from around 1865-70, possibly produced by Société Anonyme des Hauts-Fourneaux et Fonderies du Val d'Osne, to the Café Daum chair design.*

The Café Daum Chair - Model no. 4 (1850)

When Thonet designed a light and elegant chair that was also cheap, it proved an instant success. The proprietress of the Café Daum, which was a haunt of foreign correspondents and members of the military, ordered the new model with the mirror image scrolls.

Early chairs of this type still exist in a number of different variations. They are technically a step back from the innovative Liechtenstein chair as, to keep production cost down, Thonet did not use the thin rod laminates, but instead used thin, flat laminated strips for the seat and back. Even the S-shaped ornaments of the back rest are made of nine glued layers, which were bent into shape and screwed into the stile as single parts. The front legs were dowelled directly into the seat frame, which was connected to the back unit with four screws.

The model on the opposite page is the series production model, made of solid bent wood parts screwed together, which appeared in the catalogues.

The Consumer chair - Model no. 14 (1859-60)

Chair number 14 became the epitome of the cheap, mass-consumer article and, as such, stands as a symbol for 'the chair', which was to be discovered by generation after generation. It used the minimum of material but was strong and elegant, as well as having technically the best possible form for mass-production. It is regarded, mainly by architects, as the most successful industrial product of the 19th century. For more than a century it has been seen as a brilliant design by Michael Thonet, while his subsequent application of new techniques in a way ideally suited to mass-production has been just as highly regarded. In reality, however, the stylistic development of the 'chair of the century' was less clear and ingenious.

The Viennese furniture manufacturer Dannhauser had already produced a Biedermeier chair in 1820, which in form and concept must be regarded as the forerunner of chair no. 14 because it was already designed in a way suitable for industrial production. When Michael Thonet geared his work towards industrial production, decoration and time-consuming techniques had to give way before the demands of simple and fast mass-production. The consumer, or three florin chair, did not suddenly appear in 1859 as the cheapest chair available, but first ran through all the usual stages from hand-made single piece (chair no. 8) to a uniform mass-produced article (chair no. 14).

Although there were several simple bent wood chairs with double curved back rails on the market at the time, Thonet's chair no. 14 differs clearly from its competitors because of its balanced elegance. The other models have often been incorrectly seen as Thonet's experimental chair types, despite the fact that not one of them has yet been discovered bearing a Thonet stamp.

From around 1861 Thonet began to produce model no. 14 out of solid bent wood. The solid bent parts could now be screwed together, avoiding the gluing that the bent laminates had required. By 1867 at the latest, the Consumer chair no. 14 could be assembled from 6 parts, 10 screws and 2 washers.

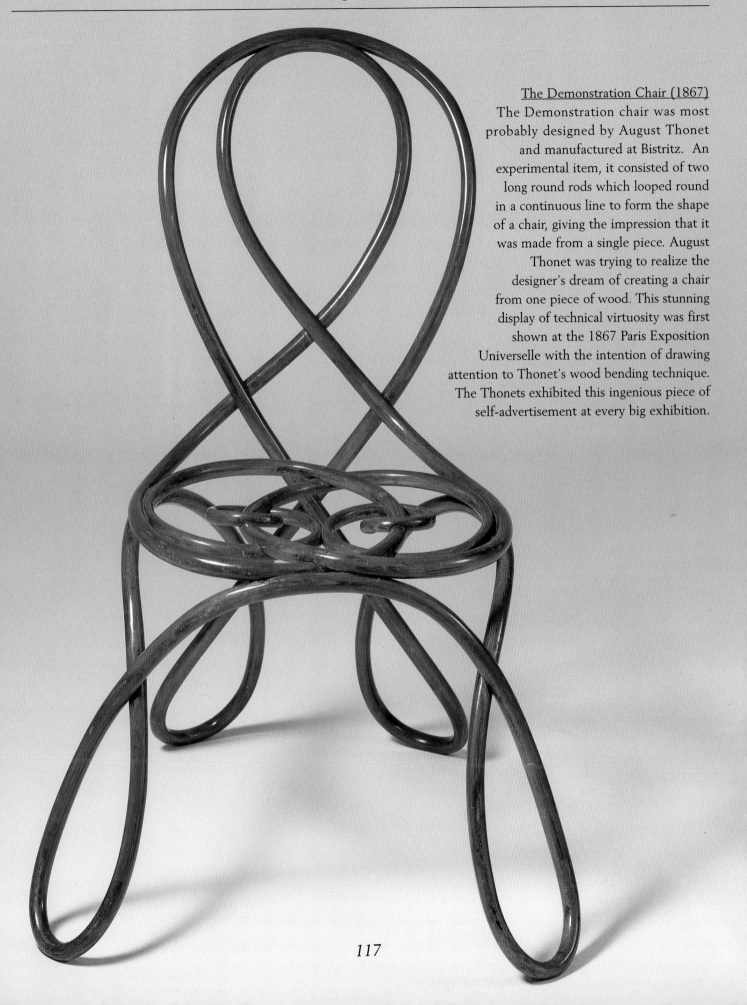

<u>The Demonstration Chair (1867)</u>
The Demonstration chair was most probably designed by August Thonet and manufactured at Bistritz. An experimental item, it consisted of two long round rods which looped round in a continuous line to form the shape of a chair, giving the impression that it was made from a single piece. August Thonet was trying to realize the designer's dream of creating a chair from one piece of wood. This stunning display of technical virtuosity was first shown at the 1867 Paris Exposition Universelle with the intention of drawing attention to Thonet's wood bending technique. The Thonets exhibited this ingenious piece of self-advertisement at every big exhibition.

The Rocking Sofa - Model no. 7500 (1883)

This rocking chaise longue - called a 'sofa' - which first appeared in Thonet's 1883 catalogue, is regarded as the most beautiful and elegant of the mass-produced 19th century bent wood designs . Its designer is unknown, but it is assumed that August Thonet, as technical director, at least had a hand in its development.

The rocking sofa is designed in long, beautifully flowing lines. The side pieces, however, do not consist of a single length of beech wood running continuously, as is usually suggested, but are constructed from two separate pieces spliced near the intersection of the arms.

The rocking sofa was not only a very comfortable piece of furniture, but also convincingly demonstrated the unique qualities of bent wood. With the increasing wealth of the middle classes, it was introduced as a piece of furniture for conservatories.

The Three Legged Chair – Model no. 81 (1906-7)

　　　This avant-garde chair with its three legs was an early forerunner of the 1920s' Vienna architect style, but its designer is not known. It is manufactured today as model no. 225P.

　　　In its minimal frame and construction it is a perfect solution for a chair. Its shape, with the two striking arcs, not only gives it elegance but also stability, so all decorative elements fulfil a clear function.

The Vienna Chair - Model no. 9 (1902-3)

Designed as Writing Desk Chair no. 9, this model was first introduced in 1902-3. It was shown at the 1925 Exposition Internationale des Arts Décoratifs in Paris and the 1927 Werkbund exhibition at the Weißenhof Siedlung in Stuttgart. Since it was both inexpensive and comfortable, it became very popular.

Le Corbusier furnished his Pavillon de l'Esprit Nouveau with model no. 9 and said of his selection: '....we believe that this chair, millions of which are in use in our continent and the two Americas, is a noble thing....'. Writing about it in 1927, Danish architect Poul Henningsen states: 'This chair completely fulfils its purpose of being a light, comfortable armchair with a low back. If an architect were to make it five times as expensive, three times as heavy and half as comfortable and a quarter as attractive, he could make his name with it.'

The Postsparkassen Stool (1905)

When the Vienna Postal Savings Bank (the 'Postsparkasse') was built, its architect Otto Wagner and his pupil Marcel Kammerer designed special furniture made out of squared bent wood in what came to be known as the 'Postsparkassen style'. The building and its furniture made design history.

The Postsparkassen stool, which Thonet later offered in his catalogues as series no. 4746, was designed by Otto Wagner for the Postal Savings Bank and used together with a desk in the main banking hall. It was constructed of five rectangular bent frames and provides excellent stability, although it is lightweight and easily transportable. There is even a handhold cut into the plywood seat.

The Wassily Chair - Model no. B3 (1925)

The first prototype of Marcel Breuer's B3 Cubist tubular steel armchair, later known as the 'Wassily', did not have the characteristic steel runners that appeared on the later series model - the final production model was screwed together. Breuer built the prototype during his spare time at the Dessau Bauhaus. It was first produced by Standard Möbel and later by Thonet, but only for a few years as during the 1930s popular taste moved away from the avant-garde towards bourgeois conformism. The B3 became a world-wide success when Gavina in Bologna re-released it in the 1960s, having named it the 'Wassily' after Kandinsky.

The Cantilever Chair - Model no. MR533 (1927)

Inspired by Mart Stam's idea of a chair without back legs, Ludwig Mies van der Rohe created a cantilever chair that far surpassed Stam's original version in both strength and swing. This elegant chair was first shown at the Werkbund exhibition at the Weißenhof Siedlung in Stuttgart. Mies van der Rohe's chair was first manufactured in tiny quantities by a very small firm in Berlin, Josef Müller/Bamberger, and from November 1932 by Thonet.

The Double Cantilever Chair - Model no. B35 (1930)

Marcel Breuer's cantilever chair on runners was first introduced in 1930 at an exhibition in Paris, as the contribution of the German Werkbund. It is one of the outstanding tubular steel designs of all time and is still manufactured today. The cantilever effect of this chair is doubly realized, in the seat and the armrests. Its originality could not be easily matched by other furniture designers and Breuer himself referred to his chair as "styleless".

Chaise Longue Model no. B306 (1928)

The furniture of Le Corbusier and his associates Pierre Jeanneret and Charlotte Perriand caused a sensation when it first appeared in exhibitions. Thonet Frères was the first to mass-produce the Le Corbusier models.

The adjustable chaise longue no. B306 was a complex design, for which Thonet's 19th century rocking sofa served as the inspiration. It was manufactured in bent chromed tubular steel and was available in Eisengarn (iron cloth), hide, leather and fabric. The design was complicated technically, and its form was determined by ergonomics - a new consideration in furniture manufacture. Thonet marketed a version which actually rocked.

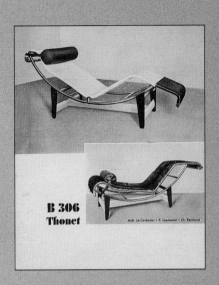

B 306
Thonet

Arch. Le Corbusier / P. Jeanneret / Ch. Perriand

CHAPTER SIX

Dating Items

As a result of Michael Thonet's early realization that a product becomes unmistakable only if it carries a proprietary name, Thonet furniture is usually marked with a paper label, a stamp or both.

Both, however, are not always to be found now - particularly on very early items manufactured before 1870. Even if an item of furniture has neither a label nor a stamp, it can still be reliably identified as Thonet from a number of other hallmarks; symbols such as a star or a sun stamped into the wood, or a variety of numbers and letters hammered into the item.

These stamps, labels and other marks are best classified into the following groups:

Early stamps	Production and assembly
Paper labels	Other labels and stamps
Later stamps	

Early stamps

There is no doubt that the earliest marks date back to 1849, the year when Michael Thonet stopped working for the Viennese cabinet maker and manufacturer of parquet flooring Carl Leistler and founded his first independent workshop in the Gumpendorf area of Vienna. The products of this workshop are marked with the stamp 'Thonet Wien Gump 396'. These stamps are found on the early items not yet produced by using solid wood bending techniques, but still made in laminated veneers.

The marking of the Thonet products only began to assume a greater significance as other cabinet makers in Vienna began to use the same technique of laminated veneers.

In the spring of 1853 the workshop at Hauptstraße 396 in Gumpendorf became too small and Thonet moved to Mollardgasse, where he began to use the stamps 'GB THONET', 'Thonet Wien' and 'GT' instead of 'Gump 396'. These stamps are to be found both on those models still made partly of laminated veneer and partly of solid bent wood, and also on the very first pieces of furniture made entirely in solid bent wood.

Next to these stamps a 'sun', a little circle with 8 rays 12mm in diameter, is often found stamped under high pressure on the underside of the seat. This 'sun' is easily confused with the 'star' marking, which was only used later in conjunction with 'Thonet' stamped into the back of the seat frame. The 'star', however, can be distinguished by its many rays, lack of an inner circle and diameter of 18mm.

Due to the fact that the underside of the laminated seat frame was flat, since the holes for the cane seat were drilled at an angle from the top and came out through the side, the stamps 'Thonet Wien Gump 396' and 'GB THONET' run diagonally across the underside of the seat frame.

ABOVE: *The 'sun' stamp, which was often stamped under high pressure on the underside of the seat on the early models.*

ABOVE: *The 'star' stamp was only used later, and in conjunction with 'THONET' stamped into the back of the seat frame.*

OPPOSITE: *Thonet logos on an anniversary envelope from Thonet, York, Pennsylvania 1980.*

ABOVE: *Early stamp used from 1849 on laminated veneer furniture from the Gumpendorf workshop in Vienna.*

LEFT & OPPOSITE: *Laminated
veneer chairs made in the
Gumpendorf workshop.*

ABOVE: *One of the stamps used between 1853 and 1857 on furniture from the Mollardgasse workshop. On early models the underside of the seat frame was flat, since the holes for the caning were drilled diagonally.*

ABOVE & BELOW: *From 1857 the holes for the cane were drilled vertically and a groove moulded between them to take the cane. This meant the marks had to be stamped lengthways. These two stamps were also used on furniture produced in the Mollardgasse workshop.*

One of the first pieces of furniture made in solid wood, without any laminated veneer.

ISLE COLLEGE
RESOURCES CENTRE

After Thonet opened his first big factory at Koritschan in Moravia in 1857, however, he used solid bent wood frames almost exclusively. The holes for the cane could now be drilled vertically through the seat frame without appreciably weakening it and, once a groove had been moulded between the holes for the cane, there was no longer room for the diagonal stamp. The mark on these pieces is therefore stamped lengthways along the grain of the wood. In addition, the 'sun' mark is to be found on almost all items stamped in this way.

Since these stamps, however, were often only superficial and uneven - and so soon became indistinguishable through usage and weather conditions - they were unsuitable for indicating the proprietary name at a glance as had been intended. The first Thonet label was therefore developed to replace these stamps.

Paper Labels

The first label was an intricate design measuring 105mm x 30mm. It said 'K.K. ausschl. priv. u landesbef. Fabriken massiv gebogener Holz-Arbeiten von Gebrüder Thonet in Wien', and had a monogram of the letter 'G' for 'Gebrüder' (Brothers) and 'T' for Thonet in the middle and the crossed initials 'GT' at each end.

It appears that Thonet began using the solid wood bending techniques described on the label in the early 1860s, although he had been granted the Austrian patent for 'solid wood bending to produce chairs and table legs' in 1856. Although definite proof of the actual date of registration of the label has not yet been found, detailed research has shown that it was first used in 1862. In official reports about Thonet's work in the 1862 London Exhibition it was stated that 'while bent wood previously consisted of several bent parts which were laminated, for two years now it has been possible to bend any contour from solid wood, which considerably improves stability and durability'. Although this doubtless originates from information provided to the exhibition commission by the company for the purposes of self-promotion, it does nonetheless help to pin down the early 1860s as the period when Thonet's production of solid bent wood furniture began.

In the years that followed, the production of the Thonet factories reached amazing heights and their work became the epitome of bent wood furniture. Now the special technique was referred to not only in the text of the first label, but in any advertisement, catalogue or other material relating to the company. This self-promotion proved so successful that by the time the second label was registered at the Chamber of Trade and Commerce on 28th July 1881, Thonet had become world famous and the reference to the production technique had therefore become unnecessary.

This second label remained in use until 1921 and is the one most commonly found on surviving pieces of Thonet furniture. It has the name 'THONET' in the middle with 'WIEN'

BELOW LEFT: *The first paper label, which was used from 1862.*

BELOW: *The second label, which was registered in 1881 but did not appear in the catalogue until 1886. This label remained in use until 1921 and is the one most commonly found on surviving Thonet furniture.*

RIGHT: *For Hungary the 'GT' became 'TT', for Thonet Testverek, and Wien was omitted.*

RIGHT: *The label for North American furniture was much larger, due to the extra information it carried.*

underneath and on either side the same crossed initials 'GT' that were on the first label. The new labels, however, were only introduced gradually as the supply of old ones was used up, so that the old label was still featured in the 1883 catalogue and the new label only appears in that of 1885.

The label was adjusted for foreign markets without changing it significantly: the label for Russia was in Cyrillic; for Hungary the initials 'GT' were replaced by 'TT' (for Thonet Testverek, Thonet Brothers in Hungarian) and 'Wien' was omitted, with the free area being filled with neutral hatching; for the North American market extensive references to the protection of patterns and designs and the quality were added on each side and the full address of the New York branch on Broadway was printed along the bottom, so that the label had to be enlarged.

RIGHT: *The third label, introduced after 1919 and officially registered in 1922. This label remained virtually unchanged until 1988.*

RIGHT: *Paper label used by Thonet Czechoslovakia ca. 1922-39, on furniture for export to France and the Colonies.*

The end of the First World War brought about the collapse of the Austro-Hungarian Empire and changed the political map of Europe. The Thonet factories were now in Czechoslovakia, Poland and Germany, so in 1919 the label was changed again. The third label simply had 'THONET' in the middle with a 'T' printed on each side - 'Wien' could, of course, no longer appear on the label. Even the furniture produced before the end of the war had to be re-labelled, in part by sticking new stamps over the old, in part by changing the stamp; in any case, all reference to Austria was removed. This third label was officially registered in 1922 and remained in use virtually unchanged until 1988.

Later Stamps

Soon after the introduction of paper labels it became clear that due to wear, dampness and weather conditions, they did not guarantee the lasting marking that was required. Many surviving items still bear the sun or other stamps, for example, but no longer have the paper label.

With the early stamps in mind, therefore, a new stamp was designed that simply said 'THONET' in capital letters about 15mm high, and which was 55mm long in all. This stamp was pressed into the underside of the seat frame, using either black or white ink, and was used in conjunction with the paper labels. As normal tools could not achieve the high pressure required for stamping, the Thonet company characteristically constructed a special machine for the job.

This stamp is mainly to be found on third generation furniture - the mass-produced sturdy models made of solid bent wood - although it does make some rare appearances on the earlier more delicate models with less flowing lines. From this fact one can draw an interesting con-clusion about the development of the models, as most of the furniture bearing this stamp comes from the second factory at Bistritz in Moravia, where the newer, sturdier bending forms were designed and used from 1862. Contemporary pieces from the first factory in Koritschan, manufactured in the old bending forms which partly still dated from the Vienna workshop, do not bear the new stamp. Koritschan slowly adapted its production, while the factories in Nagyugrócz, Wsetin and Novo-Radomsk were based from the first on Bistritz.

When the second label was introduced, the stamp too was altered. As the first stamp was

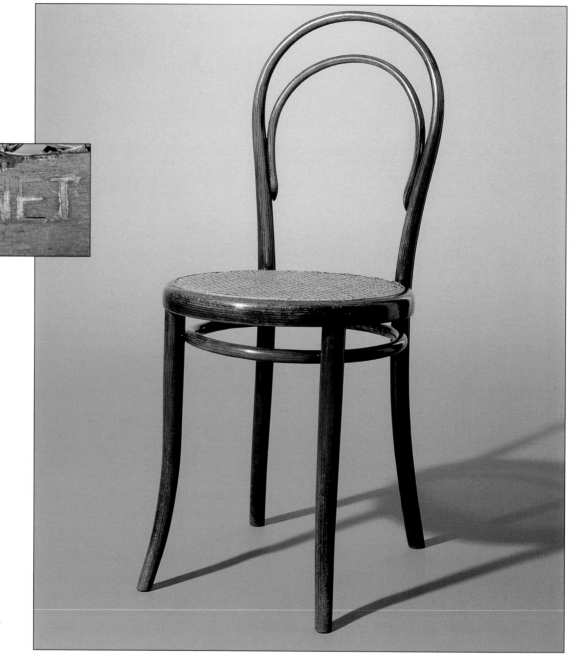

applied onto the wood without it having been prepared in any way, the mark was often incomplete and sometimes even illegible, as the inside of the seat frame was often not smooth owing to the bending process. The solution was to mould a smooth, round area, initially 42mm and later up to 60mm in diameter, onto the inside of the seat frame. The newly designed stamp, a smaller 'THONET', which was later changed to 'THONET AUSTRIA', was then applied to this smooth area. This stamp was under-laid with black paint, which led to it wrongly being called a brand. From around 1900 numbers were added to these stamps, such as 2 or 11 or 22. It is not entirely clear what these figures indicate, although they may be a reference to the year or place of production.

LEFT: *The 'THONET' stamp on the opposite page also makes a rare appearance on this earlier model.*

BELOW LEFT: *When the second paper label was introduced in the late 1880s, the 'THONET' stamp was re-designed. The new stamp was applied to a smooth area moulded on the inside of the seat frame.*

BELOW: *The new 'THONET' stamp was later revised to include the word 'AUSTRIA'. This stamp was also used in conjunction with the second paper label.*

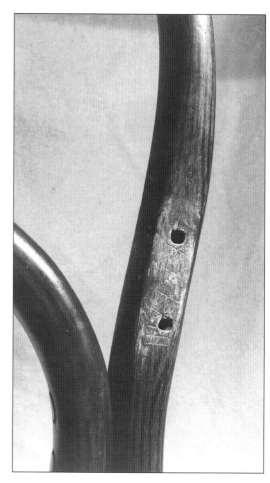

Production and assembly marks

The majority of other marks - Roman and Arabic numerals, letters or combinations of the two - fall into this group. Although it is unfortunately impossible to state anything with certainty about these markings, one can guess at their significance. The easiest to identify are the three-figure numbers moulded into the wood which are to be found on the early pieces repeated in different places, for example on the underside of the seat frame, at the top of the back legs where they join the seat frame and on the armrests on armchairs and sofas. These numbers, with the exception of those moulded on the seat frame, become invisible once the piece is assembled and were clearly supposed to mark the joints for assembly.

The rarer Roman numerals served the same purpose - every piece of the rocking chair no 3. is marked XXXXII on the joints, which was simply hammered in with a crowbar. This method of marking has its roots in traditional carpentry where the carpenter marks every piece of wood in a truss in his workshop to indicate its position for assembly. This is his only way of making sure that every piece is in the right place when the truss is erected.

Thonet numbered the pieces after the first rough assembly, before the surfaces were stained and the cane for the seat and the back was woven in. It was only later, with the development of mass-production for solid bent wood when precision became greatly improved, that all the pieces of a series became interchangeable and the marking of parts became redundant.

*Rocking chair model No. 3,
which is marked with the figures
XXXXII at every joint.*

RIGHT: *These letters*
probably indicate the factory
which produced the piece:

K-*Koritschan*
B- *Bistritz*
G-*Groß-Ugrocz (Nagyugrócz)*
W-*Wsetin*

Simple letters of the alphabet are also very common stamps, with the letters 'B', 'G', 'K' and 'W' being much more frequently used than any others. They vary from 12mm to 15mm in size and probably indicate the factory which produced the piece: B-Bistritz; G-Groß-Ugrocz (German spelling of Nagyugrócz); K-Koritschan and W-Wsetin.

ABOVE: *Paper label used by Thonet Frères in Paris, advising customers to tighten the screws from time to time.*

ABOVE: *Small brass label used by the Paris branch until around 1880.*

ABOVE: *Paper label added by the Thonet dealer in Nancy.*

ABOVE: *Interesting metal labels, either embossed or enamelled, were also occasionally used.*

Other labels and stamps

It was not only the Thonet headquarters in Vienna which was intent on marking every product in a clear and durable way; the same applied to many of the Thonet branches and some individual traders who were keen to have an additional individual label.

Perhaps the most original label was that used by Thonet Frères in Paris offering advice to the owner. It read: 'En resserrant quelquefois les vis avec lesquelles nos sièges sont assemblés, on contribue à en augmenter la durée et la solidité' (If you tighten the screws which are used to assemble our chairs from time to time, you will increase their life-span and load-bearing capacity). Until around 1880, the same Paris branch used an additional sign made of brass which was nailed underneath or on the inside of the furniture. Vallon, the Thonet dealer in Nancy, glued a round paper label with serrated edges onto the furniture which he sold. There are, in addition, a number of other metal signs, some of very interesting design, which were either embossed in brass or enamelled.

All Thonet furniture, except for the pieces produced for the 1851 Great Exhibition in London and special orders, was marked when it was produced and sold and these markings are the best way of dating the items. The numbering of models, however, is not a reliable method as it is only logical for chairs no. 1, 2 and 3 - the Café Daum chair, model no. 4, is already probably in the wrong place, and with chair no. 9 it becomes apparent that the numbering was done retrospectively and unsystematically.

OPPOSITE: *The Café Daum chair is listed as model no. 4, but model numbers are not reliable for dating items since the numbering is only logical for model nos. 1, 2 & 3.*

LEFT: *Additional enamelled label added by the Thonet dealer in Marseille.*

CHAPTER SEVEN

Care and Repair

Thonet furniture consists of pieces of bent wood which are screwed together. Even hard beech wood is hygroscopic and so changes its volume as a result of quite minor climatic changes. This will cause the screws to loosen over time and if, in addition, the chairs are used constantly and strenuously, they can become very unstable. Thonet pointed this out very early on in its catalogues and Thonet Frères added a special paper label, which was glued onto the seat frame next to the Thonet stamp and advised customers to tighten the screws from time to time.

Thonet pieces require no more care than other furniture; they should not be subjected to the elements, especially not rain, and the surface of the wood should be freshened up from time to time with simple furniture polish.

Removing dirt and grease

After years of usage, especially in restaurants and cafés, there can be a build up of dirt and grease which makes the wood look dull. This can sometimes be cleaned off with warm water, perhaps with a little washing up liquid added if the grease is heavy, using a cloth or a very soft brush. Allow to dry completely, then finish with a little furniture polish.

If the surface of the wood is matt, very dirty or greasy, the surface should be scoured along the grain with medium fine steel wool. Steel wool soaked in white spirit will dissolve any grease residue. It is then usually sufficient to merely freshen the surface up with ordinary furniture polish.

The cane does not need special care but should not be allowed to become damp during the cleaning process.

Replacing the cane

The cane seats and back rests that are a characteristic of Thonet furniture are made of rattan, a variety of climbing palm which is found in the tropical jungles of Eurasia, particularly the East Indies. There are many different types of rattan, depending on the climate and the soil, but they all have long slender stems. Although these can vary in diameter from 1.8 to 4.5mm, they maintain a high degree of uniformity throughout their length. The stems can grow as long as 182m but are cut into lengths of 4-6m for shipment. In the factory the soft core is removed and the hard and durable outer part of the stem is used for caning.

Although it is possible to buy DIY caning material, considerable experience is required to achieve a reasonable result when re-caning seats and back rests, so only an experienced basket-maker should undertake such repair work. It is also unwise to repair only part of the cane, as the new, stronger caning material can cause stress, resulting in parts of the old cane

OPPOSITE: *Child's cradle, made by J & J Kohn c.1880-90, in the process of restoration. A thick coat of white paint is being carefully removed to reveal the original black finish.*

breaking soon afterwards, which would mean repeating the whole job.

After removing the old cane completely, the seat frame is prepared by carefully rubbing away any rough lacquer or grease with medium fine steel wool. Any other repair work required should also be done at this stage. The new cane should be as close as possible in size to the old cane. The order for weaving is illustrated on page 147; take a length of cane and secure it in the first hole with a wooden peg, then proceed as illustrated, making sure that the shiny surface of the cane is facing upwards. Pull the cane taut, but avoid stretching it as some shrinkage will occur naturally as the material dries out. When the length of cane runs out, secure it with another wooden peg and begin a fresh length in the next hole. Leave the ends on the underside loose and tie them off when the weaving is complete. To finish off, select a length of beading cane and a long length of very thin cane and secure them both in one corner with a peg, the beading cane on the top and the narrow cane protruding underneath. Lay the beading cane along the edge of the weaving, then bring the narrow cane up through the next hole, over the beading cane and back down through the same hole, forming a loop to keep the beading cane in place. Carry on round the seat in the same manner, securing the ends in the last hole with a wooden peg, which should be knocked down just below the surface of the wood with a nail punch or bradawl.

Thonet usually used a cane pattern with octagonal holes, the fineness of which depends on the distance between the holes in the seat frame. The very early items have an especially fine weave, whereas the later factory produced series models have a stronger, although less fine pattern. New cane should be treated with thinned wood stain on both sides to blend in with the patina of the old wood; the colour should first be tested on a spare piece of cane. If a slight silk sheen is desired, the top surface can be treated with a matt finish varnish after staining. The varnish should be applied with a cotton wool ball – it is important to note that the application of synthetic resin with a brush runs contrary to the character of bent wood furniture and is totally wrong in all circumstances.

As the renewal of cane seats posed a considerable problem, Thonet's catalogue offered spare seat frames – already caned and with pre-bored fixing holes – which could be screwed onto the original frame once the old cane seat had been removed. Thonet's competitor, J&J Kohn, offered certain chairs with interchangeable cane frames.

RIGHT: *Spare seat frames, already caned, were offered in the Thonet catalogue.*

Rohrstuhlgeflecht aus Peddigrohr

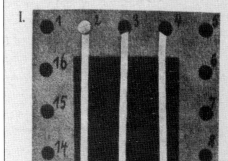

I. Aufzug
Senkrecht von
2 nach 12, 11,
3, 4, 10.

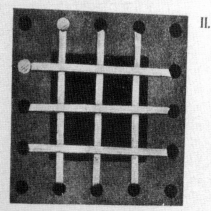

II. Aufzug
Wagrecht zurück
10—8—14—15—
7—6—16.

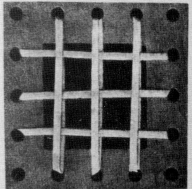

III. Aufzug
Senkrecht wie
der erste Aufzug.

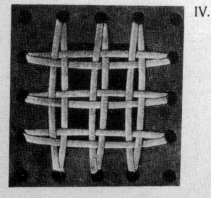

IV. Durchzug
Wagrecht,
eins auf, eins
nieder.

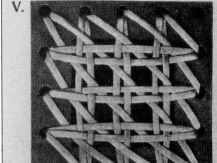

V. Durchzug
Von 1 nach 9,
10 nach 16,
15 nach 11,
12 nach 14,
wieder von
1 nach 9,
8 nach 2,
3 nach 7,
6 nach 4.

VI. Durchzug
Entgegengesetzt von
5 nach 13,
von 13 nach 4, usf.

Das Ende der Fäden wird auf
der Unterseite verknotet, indem man
das Ende zweimal um einen Faden

schlingt und durch die entstehende
Schleife zieht. Kurze Enden wer-
den mit einem Holzkeil befestigt,

LEFT: *Instructions for caning a chair seat:*

I *Vertical stringing from 2 to 12, 11, 3, 4, 10*

II *Horizontal stringing back 10, 8, 14, 15, 7, 6, 16*

III *Vertical stringing as in I*

IV *Horizontal stringing, one up, one down*

V *Stringing from:*
   1 to 9
   10 to 16
   15 to 11
   12 to 14
again from:
   1 to 9
   8 to 2
   3 to 7
   6 to 4

VI *Opposite stringing from:*
   5 to 13
   from 13 to 4 and so on.

The ends of the strands of cane are knotted on the underside by looping the end twice around the strand and pulling it through the loop. Short ends are secured with a wooden wedge.

RIGHT: *This J & J Kohn chair had an interchangeable cane seat.*

FAR LEFT: *To repair small splits and chips, first cut out the damaged area.*

LEFT: *Fill the hole with wood filler, then sand down with fine sandpaper and stain to blend in with the old surface.*

Simple repair work

Dirty or rough surfaces and small splits or chips are easy to repair. If, as is often the case, the surface of the wood is matt and the lacquer is porous and rough, again the wood should be scoured hard along the grain with medium fine steel wool. If this does not prove sufficient, very fine sand paper (grade 200) can be used. This, however, must be done carefully to avoid damaging areas of the old surface that are still intact. The surface can then be freshened up with ordinary furniture polish - unless the old surface is very worn, in which case its matt silken sheen should be restored with matt varnish. Restoration with shellac should be left to a specialist, and again it is important to note that synthetic resin should never be used, nor should the finish be applied with a brush.

Slight splits and chips are repaired by cutting out the damaged area and filling the hole with wood filler. When the filler is hard it should be sanded down with fine sand paper and stained to blend in with the old surface.

Woodworm are the great enemy of wooden furniture and are indicated by small holes the size of pinheads. To find out if the woodworm are still alive, place the item onto a black surface and blow away any wood borings. If fresh ones have appeared the following day, there is no doubt that the woodworm are still alive and kicking. Many different woodworm remedies are available, but they all contain strong poisons and so should be used only if there is no alternative. The best treatment for woodworm is to have the furniture disinfected in a special chamber which is heated to 60-70°C. The high temperature kills every organism in the item, but does not affect the bent wood.

RIGHT: *Detail showing glued-in dowels which hide fixing screws.*

RIGHT: *The punches used to cut new dowels from thin strips of beech wood come in different sizes.*

Restoration of severe damage

Repairing breaks, shortened legs, parts riddled with woodworm, broken screws and bends that have lost their curvature requires practice, experience and the right tools and should only be tackled by an expert. Before starting restoration or repair work on severe damage, a decision must be made on whether the piece needs to be taken apart. To do this requires the correct tools - the screwdriver must be of the right size and must have sharp edges to prevent it sliding off and damaging the item, and a suitable key is required to undo the screws on the back legs.

When dismantling a Thonet chair, it is important to avoid mixing up the components with parts from other chairs. Since every item of Thonet furniture was individually assembled by hand the screw holes, for example, are in a slightly different position on each item. Every piece should be marked during disassembly so that it can be replaced just as it was; if, for example, the foot ring is not replaced in exactly the same position, the screw holes will not match up.

Where they would otherwise be visible, the screws are sunk deep into the wood and covered by glued-in dowels. To unfasten these screws, the dowels must first be removed with a sharp, thin-edged screwdriver. Although the dowels usually break in the process, great care is nonetheless needed to avoid damaging the surrounding wood. When reassembling the chair, these dowels can be replaced with new ones of the same diameter. The new dowels should be cut from a strip of beech wood 2-3mm thick with a punch, and should be inserted so that the grain of the dowel matches the grain of the furniture. If, as is often the case, the screws are so tight that they break when any attempt is made to loosen them, the problem should then be left to a specialist to avoid considerable damage to the item.

Missing screws should ideally be replaced by matching them with old screws taken from bent wood pieces which are beyond restoration. If this is not possible, new screws can be made by taking a modern screw longer than the original and shortening it with a metal saw where it runs into a point. This will create a screw with a front section as strong as the original.

Large breaks or cracks should not be filled with wood filler; instead the damaged area should be sawn off in the direction of the grain, to ensure that the remaining cross section is sufficiently stable. Then take a piece of furniture beyond restoration and cut a replacement piece from a corresponding area with a similar curvature. This replacement piece should be roughly adapted to the item to be restored, glued in position and held in place with clamps. The following day the repair can be worked on with a rasp, file and sandpaper until it matches the original exactly. After this the surface should be finished as described in the section on page 157, 'Treating the wood surface: varnishing and polishing'.

Bent parts - such as the armrests of chairs - which have lost some of their curvature can be bent back up to a point. To do this the part must be removed from the chair. To prevent it becoming even more out of shape, a template corresponding to its existing shape should be made by cutting out a negative from a suitably sturdy plank. The bent wood piece is then fitted

ABOVE: *Illustration of one of the machines used to drill fixing holes by hand.*

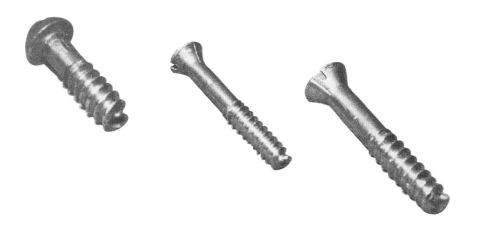

LEFT: *New screws can be made by taking a modern screw longer than the original and cutting it back with a metal saw at the point.*

ABOVE: *The slender bent wood of the back rest on this rare collector's item is badly broken in several places.*

ABOVE: *The back rest is removed and the larger damaged areas are cut out and repaired with new wood. This is then gently and carefully sanded into shape.*

ABOVE: *Small chips are repaired with wood filler and broken parts re-glued. The back rest is then cleaned and re-assembled.*

into the template and both of them soaked in water overnight. Meanwhile, a new template should be made that corresponds exactly to the required curvature. Remove the part from the water, take it out of the old template and bend it into the new one - which can be quite strenuous work. The piece should then be left to dry for one or two days before removing it from the template. After the surface has been refinished, the part can be replaced. This procedure is, however, only effective on parts that have only slightly lost their curvature.

If a piece is badly out of shape it must be restored in the same way as it was originally made by Thonet, which is really only practical for professional restorers carrying out art restoration of Thonet furniture. A mould must first be constructed and the bending is then effected with the help of a metal strip which stops the wood splitting.

Reconstructing destroyed or missing parts

The reconstruction of major destroyed or missing parts of furniture should normally be done by a specialist - especially if they are bent parts, as it is extremely difficult to do such work in a private workshop. It is usually only worthwhile to carry out this sort of extensive work on very rare collector's items and museum pieces. Ideally, the replacement part will be taken from a similar piece of furniture which is beyond restoration but, if the items are very rare, finding such a piece would be extremely unlikely. The true collector, however, never gives up and is always on the look-out for suitable pieces.

LEFT: *The back rest is replaced on the chair and stained and polished to match the original finish.*

It is, however, much easier to reconstruct smaller pieces of bent wood using the Thonet method, even in a collector's workshop, provided that a sample is available to construct the template. This template should be made of hardwood and room should be allowed for Michael Thonet's well-known invention: a flat metal strip with screw clamps at each end to stop the wood splitting. The rod to be bent should be cut to length and the correct cross section and soaked in water for two to three days. After the metal strip has been attached, it can then be bent over the template and secured there. When the rod has dried into shape, finer work such as diagonal cuts and surface treatment can be carried out.

Legs that are too short because they have splintered or broken off, or are riddled with woodworm, are not too difficult to restore to their proper length. The damaged part of the leg should be sawn off at an angle to make a cut about 8-10cm in length. A replacement piece can then either be taken from a spare old chair leg, or cut from a length of beech wood of corresponding cross section. The end of the replacement piece should be cut to the same angle and to glue the leg effectively both parts must be perfectly adjusted; stability can be increased by connecting both sections with a hidden dowel. After the glue has dried the replacement piece should be adjusted by filing and sanding, and once the leg has been re-assembled it can be shortened to its final length.

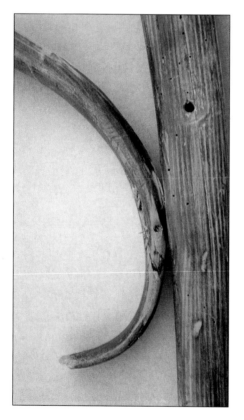

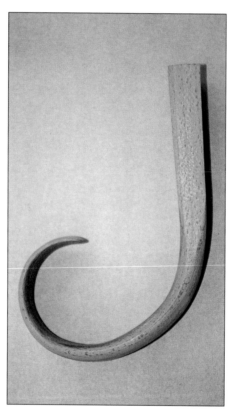

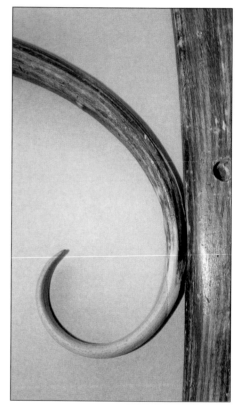

ABOVE: *The end of this piece of curved bent wood has been broken off.*

ABOVE: *A new piece is cut from beech wood and bent to the required curvature.*

ABOVE: *The new piece is fixed to the original bent wood part and the last detailed shaping done with fine sandpaper before staining and finishing.*

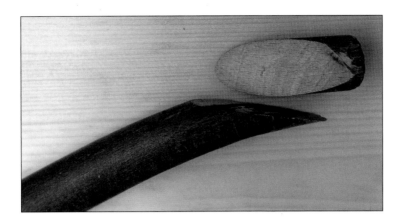

LEFT: *The end of a damaged leg is sawn off at an angle to give a larger fixing area.*

LEFT: *A new piece is cut roughly to size, either from a spare chair leg or from beech wood of a corresponding cross section. The new piece is cut to the same angle and a dowel is added to give the join extra strength. A corresponding hole is drilled in the original leg.*

LEFT: *The new piece is attached before being cut to length.*

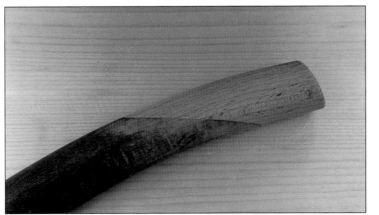

LEFT: *The new piece is carefully sanded down to the correct size and shape, before staining and finishing.*

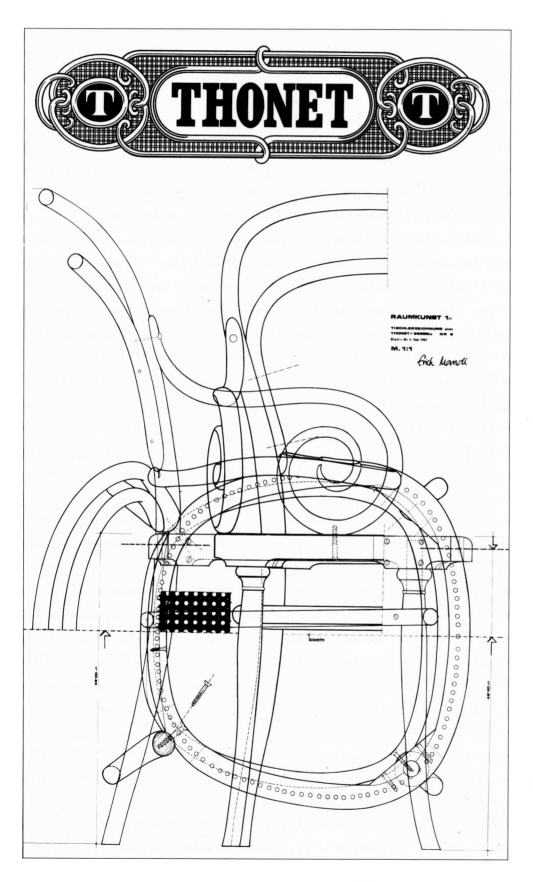

Treating the wood surface: varnishing and polishing

Perhaps the greatest danger associated with work on Thonet furniture is 'over-restoring'. The surface of even the early mass-produced Thonet furniture was treated very differently from the modern restorers' usual methods. The beech wood was usually stained in a colour that could be selected by the customer from catalogues offering everything from natural wood to mahogany, walnut, oak and black. These surfaces were homogeneously one-tone, except for the interesting palisander variation, which was achieved by rolling dark paint lengthways along the wood with a comb-like rubber roller to produce the effect of a strong lengthways grain. The wood was then stained reddish-brown so that it looked like real palisander. After staining and the application of an undercoat, the wood was varnished with a shellac solution, the exact proportions of which were the closely guarded secret of each bent wood furniture manufacturer. The finish of mass-produced items was applied after assembly by spraying.

When restoring a Thonet piece, it is crucial to achieve a surface and overall impression which is as much in keeping with the character of the original piece as possible. Parts of the old surface should be kept to match the new surface to, if at all possible, so that the whole piece can be stained; the new part will absorb the stain while the old will remain unchanged. After applying the undercoat - linseed oil or a solvent-based undercoat - a shellac or matt varnish should be applied. This can be done with a cotton wool ball using medium pressure along the grain to produce a lively patina. Never work on Thonet furniture with paint or a brush.

If one tries to achieve a finish as true as possible to the original when repairing or restoring, then this time-intensive work will doubtless pay off and the Thonet collector will continue to get enjoyment from his piece for many years.

RIGHT: *Chair from the suite manufactured for Count Palffy in the mid 19th century.*

Index

ISLE COLLEGE
RESOURCES CENTRE